AND I AM AFRAID OF
MY DREAMS

AND I AM AFRAID OF MY DREAMS

Wanda Półtawska

Translated from the Polish by
Mary Craig

HIPPOCRENE BOOKS, INC.
New York

Publication of this volume was made possible by a generous grant from the Polish Army Veterans Association of America.

Hippocrene Books paperback edition, 2013.

For information, address:
HIPPOCRENE BOOKS, INC.
171 Madison Avenue
New York, NY 10016
www.hippocrenebooks.com

ISBN 10: 0-7818-1303-4
ISBN 13: 978-0-7818-1303-7

Printed in the United States of America.

TRANSLATOR'S ACKNOWLEDGMENT

To my friend, Sister Jessica of the Assumptive Order, who many years ago gave me her Polish dictionaries, Wanda Półtawska's two books, and a translation she had already made of "*I Boję Się Snów.*" It was not until 1985 when I had made reasonable progress in Polish that I decided to read both books for myself. Having done so, I was bowled over by them.

PUBLISHER'S NOTE

The original edition of Wanda Półtawska's *And I Am Afraid of My Dreams* was published in Polish in 1961. In 1987, this English translation by Mary Craig was published in the U.K., and in 1989, Hippocrene Books published the first American edition of Półtawska's remarkable memoir.

Now over twenty years later and with a generous grant from The Polish Army Veterans Association of America, Hippocrene Books is able to bring Wanda Półtawska's memoir back into print. Her story is as relevant and moving today as when she originally penned it in the early months after her release from the Nazi concentration camp almost seventy years ago. Our hope is that this testament to resilience, bravery, and humanity will continue to inspire and teach a new generation of readers.

Hippocrene Books also thanks Maria Chrusciel for her tireless assistance with this project.

AUTHOR'S NOTE

To the reader of today and of tomorrow:

You might think that no one cares anymore about what happened during the Second World War, so many years ago. But that is not the case. Even though the first generation born after the war, our children, did not want to hear about it, the next generation, our grandchildren, not only want to listen but they are searching for knowledge about this period. They voraciously read this book and keep asking, "how could anyone have survived something like that?"

What are they searching for in this book and what do they find?

I think that they are looking for the truth about man, and what they find are values, values which are disappearing from our world, although they are immortal.

My story about our youth shows something that the so-called world of "western civilization" is unable to demonstrate—the fact that human nature can stretch between heroism and bestiality.

My generation survived the shock of finding out that man can become inhumane, and this discovery might have led to despair, if it were not for the fact that those times also demonstrated that man can become in some sense superhuman—a hero. If he can become a monster, he can also become a saint, and this is as true today as it was then.

So my story about the experiences of my generation is a warning for young people, because everybody can become like a member of the Gestapo, or on the other hand, like Maksymilian Kolbe, or the woman I describe in my book, Wladka Dabrowska, who was ready to give her life to save that of a young girl, Krysia Czyz. My account is a witness to crime and heroism. It demonstrates the strength of the human spirit, the meaning of faith in God and faith in man. It shows the different forms of beauty: the beauty of friendship and patriotism; the beauty of nature, in a flower rediscovered in a single stem of lilac or in the view of the silhouette of trees on the horizon; the beauty of a poem; and the healing value of humor.

Against the background of my story, the full dimension of the human being is revealed and it prompts the reader to reflect: be careful, because it could happen that you will not even notice when you become insensitive to human misery, when you have become like an SS-man. Think about it!

After many years of working as a psychiatrist I can say that this book helps me in my work with young people. When they read it, they start to think, and that is why I believe it should be given to succeeding generations. The values that you find in it are universal and unchanging. Every human person can become more or less humane—and humanity is not less threatened today than it was during the time of this story.

Wanda Półtawska
Kraków, Poland
2012

PREFACE

Niema złego co by na dobre nie wyszło.
There is no evil that cannot be turned into good.

—Polish proverb

Do not fear those who kill the body but cannot kill the soul;
rather, fear the one who can destroy both soul and body.

—Good News by St. Matthew 10:28

Wanda Półtawska's saga encapsulates Poland's millennial history as lived in a woman's soul. She is a stark witness to the repeated failure of Poland's Western (and Eastern) neighbors over centuries to imprison the nation's soul, exile its citizenry, occupy or destroy family homes, reduce the people to submission, rewrite its history textbooks, and even erase the country from the map.

The deteriorating daily conditions of Wanda's three-year cruel "animalization" tapped a native strength within Wanda and her fellow Polish women, rural or city bred, blue-blooded or not, university-degreed or taught by their mothers and families. It goes light years beyond "being tough," strong-minded, or having a stiff upper lip. It is more penetrating than personal integrity. It goes beyond "the power of positive thinking," ingenuity, or cunning. It is an ingenious journey over endless, tattered, ripping rope bridges. It climbs over crags of despair under countless seasons of clouds without "silver linings." Resilience is bred by communion. Resilience is climbing beyond human capability, to catch a fleeting glance of a sunflower or mountaintop after each put down; it is deciding to be a victim, yet never victimized; reaching out to others and choosing not to hate or blame, but instead looking for some good rather than a scapegoat; digging beyond the expanseless depths of organized injustice and electing to suffer, yet never aimlessly; trying to understand rather than fight the evil which only fears truth. It is risking punishment for embroidering the White Eagles rather than welcoming the dark abyss accessible only on a bier of high intensity wires.

How did these women do this? They lived day-to-day knowing the picture (icon) of their Mother, Queen of the Bright Mountain, is also scarred, her cheeks never masked by makeup. Starving, they made prayer beads of meager sawdust-infused bread rations. Their spirits pushed to insanity, they refused death. Their bruised souls did not collapse with each broken body. And after this war, occupied by atheistic Communism, their Church was the first to forgive Germans for Nazi atrocities on their soil and bodies.

Moreover, Wanda's personal healing was a fruit of her resilient soul. She penned these most treacherous three years of her bodily-dying. Her nightmares ended after entering every last throbbing wound into this memoir. This survivor did what few would even hear of—she re-opened the plaster cast of her scientific, compulsory, systematic, calculated, antiseptic dying. Originally intended only for her, these painful pages literally give the reader life, her life.

The resilience, rather than resistance, of these Polish women-guinea-pigs collapsed a high-tech, political extermination system. Poland again outlived the hands of avaricious neighbors, as Nazism and Communism in time fell on their own faces.

Rev. Dr. Czesław M. Krysa
September, 2012

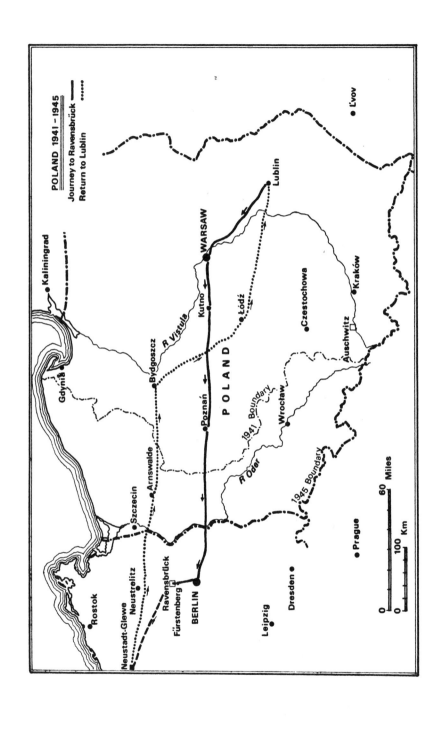

TRANSLATOR'S FOREWORD

I remember my first encounter with a group of men and women who had survived the Nazi concentration camps. It was such a devastating shock to my system that I felt I had been turned upside down and shaken. It happened in 1960, fifteen years after the final capitulation of Nazism. I had grown up during the war and like everybody else in Britain had seen the horrifying pictures taken when the British Army liberated Belsen camp. Those pictures were more than most of us could bear, and so we found a variety of reasons for dismissing them from our minds as quickly as possible. For how was it possible that human beings should do such things to other human beings? Were we perhaps all capable of such terrible inhumanity? Better by far not to follow that line of thought to its logical conclusion! Better to shut it out completely.

"We should forgive and forget," we magnanimously asserted, not understanding that neither the forgetting nor the forgiving were ours to give. Others found it more comfortable to deny that the camps had existed at all – though how they could maintain this belief in the face of the mounting evidence is a considerable mystery.

But even those who did not actually deny the very existence of the camps failed, for the most part, to understand what they really represented. It is hard to imagine the unimaginable. There is to this day a vague idea that the concentration camps were some kind of internment enclosure, unpleasant no doubt, but no different in kind from other places of internment manned by other tyrants in other lands. There was little realisation that it was in these camps that the inhuman Nazi philosophy was given its fullest expression. The Nazis, those self-styled Aryan supermen with ambitions to rule the world, had long since

7

discarded the Judaeo-Christian belief in the value of each and every human life. In its place they had substituted the principle that certain categories of human beings were actually non-persons, 'useless mouths' with no rights of any kind: not even to life.

Beginning, in the 1930s in Germany itself, with the licensed euthanasia of the mentally-retarded and the mentally-ill, the Nazis progressed, slowly but inexorably, through the elimination of their own physically substandard, socially undesirable and terminally-ill Aryans to the extermination of millions of such 'inferior' species as Jews, Russians, Gypsies and Poles. Since these were non-persons, they could be battered, starved, degraded, experimented on and exterminated at whim. In the concentration camps, millions of helpless human beings were gassed, frozen, drowned or burned to death, subjected to fatal decompression experiments, or injected with diseased bacilli, all in the name of medical research. In the words of prosecuting counsel at the medical war crimes trials at Nuremberg, the crimes were: 'so calculated, so malignant and so devastating that civilisation cannot tolerate their being ignored because it cannot survive their being repeated'. And this is the lesson we are in danger of forgetting.

The Final Solution was being prepared not only for the Jews but for the Slavs and Gypsies too. Had the war not ended when it did – at a time when the gas ovens and crematoria were only just achieving peak operational efficiency – the history of Eastern Europe might have been very different. As it is, six million, twenty-eight thousand Polish citizens died, ninety per cent of them in prisons and concentration camps. More than half were non-Jewish.

The Nazi occupation of Poland in the years 1939–1945 was the most vicious and brutal the world has ever known – and the Polish resistance movement perhaps the best organised and most heroic. It was supported by almost the entire population. There were very few Polish traitors, and no Fifth Column as existed in other occupied countries, eager and ready to form puppet regimes. The Poles were starved of food, beaten, dragged from the streets as hostages, deported to labour camps or sent off in droves to the concentration camps which were set up in large numbers in that unfortunate country. The most minor offence – or sometimes merely being in a certain place at the wrong time – merited instant deportation or arrest. Everyone was vulnerable. We in the British Isles who have never known the horrors of occupation by a foreign power have always suffered from a failure of the imagination in this respect. Our minds cannot encompass what is alien to our experience. I remember once, when I was a reporter with BBC Radio, waiting my turn to record an interview with an Auschwitz survivor who had written a book about the resistance movement in the camp. In front of me was a fair-haired, cheerful-looking young chap. "Tell me," he said, holding out his mike to the man from Auschwitz, "tell me some of the funny things that happened in the camp. Our readers don't want to be depressed by horrors." And there is another memory too, second-hand but none the less impressive. An organisation with which I was connected used to provide an annual holiday for the 'guinea-pigs' – people on whom medical experiments had been performed in the camps – and various entertainments would be laid on for them. At one party to which the group was invited, a 'guinea-pig' found herself talking to a middle-aged Englishwoman. "And what did you do during the war, my dear?" "I was in a concentration camp." "Oh, you naughty girl!" came the coy reply. "Whatever did you do to deserve that?"

An eye-witness told me that story the day after I had arrived on my first visit to a Home for concentration camp survivors in East Anglia. She told me also about Wanda Półtawska, a 'guinea-pig' from Ravensbrück who, when seemingly at the point of death reached an incredibly brave decision; she vowed to become a doctor if she survived the camp. I was haunted by Wanda's story and, though I had not met her, I used it years later in my book, *Blessings*, to illustrate the triumph of the human spirit even in the darkest and most appalling circumstances. A few months after finishing that book, in October 1978, I was asked to go to Poland to prepare a biography of the newly-elected

9

Polish Pope, the former Cardinal Karol Wojtyła of Kraków. On that occasion a mutual friend arranged for me to stay with Wanda Półtawska and her husband, Andrzej, both of them close friends of the new Pope. And so at last we met.

At the beginning of 1941, Wanda, the daughter of a post-office clerk in Lublin, was just nineteen. When the Germans had conquered Poland in September 1939 she had still been at school, hoping to study Polish Language and Literature at the University and eventually become a writer. But in Nazi-occupied Poland, all higher (and most lower) education was forbidden, and Wanda was unable to take her final school examinations. As a keen Girl Guide, she had helped organise field kitchens and first aid for the sick and wounded. When the fighting was over, and the subjugation of the Polish people began, like many of the Girl Guides she was actively involved as a courier for the burgeoning but as yet unco-ordinated Resistance. It was for the heinous crime of carrying letters and orders to the various Resistance groups that in February 1941 Wanda was arrested. She was taken first to Gestapo headquarters where she was badly beaten, then to Lublin Castle where she was thrown into a cell with prostitutes and other criminals; and finally to Ravensbrück concentration camp where ninety-two thousand women and children died in conditions of unimaginable inhumanity. It would be more than four years before she saw her home again. The Lublin girls, unaware that they had already been condemned to death, were one of the main groups from whom the Nazis selected their victims for medical experimentation. Wanda, for example, had diseased bacilli injected into her bone marrow, for no other reason than to see how the human body would 'cope'. She survived. Many of her companions did not.

When she returned from Ravensbrück in the late spring of 1945, Wanda was tormented by nightmares about the camp, and to such an extent that she dared not let herself sleep. A trusted friend and former teacher advised her to write everything down; and when she had followed this advice, she at last found the sleep that had so long eluded her. Having served its purpose, the manuscript was put into a drawer and stayed there for fifteen years, until 1960 when she was persuaded to have it published. When *And I am Afraid of my Dreams* first appeared in Poland, a student wrote and asked Wanda if what she had written was really true. "If only it were not," she replied.

After the war, she was true to her resolve to become a doctor. She qualified as a physician in 1951, and went on to study psychiatry, in her eyes the most humane of all branches of medicine, since the psychiatrist 'helps the individual to become a mature person who is aware of his or her humanity'. She concentrated mainly on juvenile psychiatry and on sexual problems; and in this capacity was able to help many of the unfortunate 'Auschwitz children', the deeply-traumatised children and young people who had been born in the concentration camps or had spent their formative years there.

Until her retirement some years ago, Wanda Półtawska worked in the psychiatric clinic of Kraków's Medical Academy, and in a special out-patients' advisory centre for problem children at Kraków's Jagiellonian University. In 1947 she married Andrzej Półtawski (now Professor of Philosophy in Warsaw's Theological Academy), and they have four daughters, two of them doctors, two still studying Art in Kraków.

While caring for a pregnant unmarried girl some time in the late 1950s Wanda sought the help of a young priest, Karol Wojtyła. It was the start of a lifelong friendship. When Karol Wojtyła became Archbishop of Kraków, he founded a Family Institute in the city and placed Wanda Półtawska in charge. As Pope John Paul II he has continued to take a great interest in this Institute, and both Wanda and her husband Andrzej are frequent visitors to Rome as members of the Papal Commission on Family Matters. They remain two of Pope John Paul's closest friends.

Today when she looks back on the Ravensbrück years, Wanda does not, for all its horror, regret the experience. Ravensbrück, she says, taught her many things. Not least, it daily brought her face to face with imminent death and made her understand that, for a Christian, all life is a preparation for life after death. She came to understand the real meaning of freedom, that interior freedom of the spirit which soars above external circumstances and cannot be destroyed. "I never lost that interior freedom," she says. It is a remarkable claim, but one borne out on every page of this remarkable record of courage and faith.

The third lesson was the hardest of all to learn, in that place of unparalleled cruelty where for years she was starved, beaten, humiliated and degraded. In spite of all this, she came to appreciate that "there is some good in every human being, no matter how bad he or she appears. One must search for that good seed, however small, cherish it and help it to grow. We should never divide people into categories of good and bad. The dividing line between good and evil lies within ourselves, within each and every one of us."

Certain traumas remain. In another, later book, she tells of a letter from a Ravensbrück survivor in Canada describing the sudden irrational impulses to which she is prone. In reply, Wanda recalled her own: the panic fear that gripped her every time she entered the new staff club room in her clinic, with its grey-blue striped walls reminding her inescapably of those massed ranks of women in grey-blue prison stripes standing to attention for hours on end during the endless morning and evening roll-calls. Voices speaking German remained another source of uncontrollable terror. She tells of a glorious day in the mountains when she is at peace with the world and revelling in its beauty. Suddenly a harmless group of Scouts passes nearby, speaking German; Wanda begins to tremble uncontrollably, her day in ruins. "The sun was still shining, yet a shadow had fallen across it. I could stay there no longer. I got up and walked away." It was a force stronger than reason, she said, something beyond the reach of the strongest effort of will, something utterly inescapable. When she returned to the clinic next day, she was asked to act as interpreter for some foreign visitors – in German. "I do not like the German language," she demurred. Her professor murmured an explanation to the visitors. "But," began one of them, looking puzzled, "you *are* a psychiatrist, after all." Wanda did not wait for him to finish. She interrupted with a single word, and it was not in German. "Stigmata," she said – and walked away.

Stigmata such as hers, both physical and mental, are inevitable. But they are overlaid by a striking courage and a profound confidence in the value of each individual life. It is as though, having looked death and destruction in the eye so often, she has learned the secret of living: to reach out to each other, to be responsible for each other. It is the spirit I have met so often in those who have plumbed the depths of human suffering, and which is testimony to the unsuspected hidden goodness of human beings driven to the limits of endurance. There is an echo here of Viktor Frankl, a survivor of Buchenwald, whose book *Man's Search for Meaning* has become a sought-after spiritual power-house. 'We who lived in concentration camps,' he wrote, 'can remember the [ones] who walked through the huts comforting others, giving away their last piece of bread. They may have been few in number, but they offer sufficient proof that everything can be taken from a [human being] but one thing: the last of the human freedoms – to choose one's attitude in any given set of circumstances, to choose one's way . . .'

Wanda Półtawska's memoir is a powerful and moving illustration of that ultimate freedom. In these pages we see humanity at its worst, but also at its incomparable best. It is, as she is careful to insist, not a definitive account of life in Ravensbrück, but one woman's authentic testimony to her own experience. She has no axe to grind, just a determination to be as truthful as she knows how, and thus to exorcise her demons. It is a personal diary, a single priceless insight into a dark period of human history which we might well prefer to forget but which it might be wiser to try to understand. We ignore it at our collective peril.

MARY CRAIG,
March 1986

13

AUTHOR'S FOREWORD

I wrote down this memoir of the concentration camp in June and July 1945, immediately after my return, and until January 1961 it lay in a drawer, as it was not intended for publication. I wrote it for an entirely different reason which I perhaps ought to explain since it illuminates the very personal way in which it is written.

I returned home on 28 May 1945, after a journey lasting twenty days – and within hours I made a terrifying discovery: every day, or rather, every night, I dreamed of Ravensbrück. The dreams were so frighteningly realistic that I was nightly reliving the appalling reality of the camp.

In the camp I had sometimes dreamed of home, and the awakening from such a dream was certainly one of the hardest experiences to bear. But now, when it was all over, it was the other way round. I was at home, and my dreams were of the camp. I dreamed the same dream every night, over and over again. I don't know how it was possible for anyone to dream so much in the course of a single night.

I fought off sleep as long as I could – and spoke to no one about what was happening. Eventually I was in such an overwrought state that I would not even go to bed. I couldn't bear those dreams about the camp . . .

For a long time I wondered who to tell. I couldn't confide in those closest to me; they would be too upset. And I knew that my being in the camp had already caused them more than enough pain. Then one day I felt so utterly exhausted that I decided that something would have to be done.

On 23 June, my first Name Day* back at home, a crowd

* In Poland people are named after a saint and honour that Saint's Day. It is a more important celebration than their own birthday.

14

of people and a sea of flowers greeted me. Towards the day's end, a kindly, grey-haired old lady came to see me: my former school-teacher. I found myself telling her that I couldn't understand it at all, that I should have survived the camp and yet be unable to tolerate my dreams . . . Did that seem to her in any way abnormal?

She didn't comment that day, but returned two days later with the news that she had consulted a psychiatrist friend about my situation. The man had said I should tell the whole story to someone I could trust.

There were plenty of people whom I trusted, but I didn't want to tell them about the camp. I shook my head. No, it wasn't possible; there were no words to describe such a traumatic experience. Besides, who was there to tell? My elderly parents? My sisters? Perhaps if I'd had a brother, a strong man . . . But I hadn't.

My old teacher didn't give up. Almost as an afterthought, she said, "You know, you really ought to try and write it all down. Perhaps it might help."

At first I resisted the suggestion. But that night, when I was once again afraid of my dreams, I started to write . . . After that I continued to write, but only at night.

One sunlit morning in July or possibly August 1945, I came to the end of my story, and put the manuscript in a drawer. That night, for the first time since my return, I enjoyed a dreamless sleep.

I wrote a brief note to my old teacher to thank her for her suggestion and to say that it had worked.

Since then, though I have sometimes dreamed of the camp with the painful clarity of those early days, it has only happened at periods of extreme exhaustion. The dreams are an advance warning that I need to let up and take a rest.

Ten years after I wrote it I told someone else about this memoir, and five years after that I was persuaded to have it published. I looked it over . . . it seemed to me too intimate, too macabre. So I removed a few paragraphs. The gaps they left behind seemed eloquent enough.

Twenty years have passed since the events described here, and I can look back on them quite dispassionately now. The stigmata have now faded and in a few days it will be the twentieth anniversary of my arrest: 17 February 1941.

KRAKÓW
10 February 1961

1

I shall try to describe it, though I honestly don't know whether that is possible. I don't believe I shall find the right words. And how could anyone who didn't live through that place understand what it was like? Thousands of women survived Ravensbrück concentration camp, but their experience was quite different from ours. By 'ours' I mean the 'guinea-pigs', or, as we say in Polish – *króliky* – the 'rabbits'.

But the point is not the actual experience so much as my own response to it. I need to sort it out and get a proper perspective on it.

I can't plunge straight into the Ravensbrück saga. I must go back and begin at the beginning . . . Back to the evening when I was studying with Nata, and a man's voice, hostile, alien, but speaking in Polish, called out from the hallway, "Which of you girls is Wanda?"

That is how it all began. I stood up and went out – and I have only just returned, after six months in prison and four years in a concentration camp. There were two men waiting for me in the hallway, and two more at the gate. "Four men to fetch one girl," I thought with scorn.

I came through the interrogation with flying colours, although to be honest, I did have one moment of blind fear. On arrival, they put me in a dark cellar, and until they took me upstairs I suffered torments of the imagination. I imagined – I don't know why – that they were going to tear out my finger-nails with pliers; and I sat on the floor in the dark, trembling with fright. When, at two in the morning, they took me into a lighted interrogation room, I made a careful scrutiny of the battleground and satisfied myself that there were no pliers or suchlike around. After that, I felt quite calm and ready to behave like a fictional heroine. In any case, the interrogation lasted only a few days. I felt pleased with myself and at ease with my conscience; I hadn't said a word more than I'd intended, and hadn't given anyone away. I had the feeling throughout that *I* was in control of the questioning, not the Germans. They assumed as a matter of course that anything I told them after a beating must be true, for how could a girl who had just been tortured refrain from telling all she knew. So I took care to tell them nothing beforehand.

True enough, on one occasion I had to hold my tongue and be silent, simply because I had finally run out of likely stories and could think of nothing to say. The interrogator would bend over me and say, very politely: "Child, it's such a shame. I could be a father to you. Just treat me right, and I'll do the same for you." I didn't deign to reply. This went on for hours, though to me it seemed like an eternity, and was as horrible in its way as the physical torture. At last, when he got weary of this kind of persuasion, I was taken to a dark room whose doors opened on to a brightly-lit hall where the most recent arrivals were being questioned. My tormentor (as I mentally called him) held a revolver at my back and threatened to shoot me if I spoke. I had no intention of saying anything. On the contrary, I wanted to hear what was going on. So, with a gun at my back, I found out who was saying what, and why I had been arrested. To this day, no one knows that I listened in on my colleagues. I was delighted, for at last I knew what to say. In my youthful idealism, I even credited my tormentor with having taken me there specially so as to make things easier for me, though future events did not bear out this belief.

On the way back from these 'investigations', I met Marylka Walciszewska on the stairs. A tall, slender girl, she looked at me and said in a loud voice: "Don't forget, just blame it all on me." I smiled. I no longer needed to blame anyone, for I had discovered exactly what they knew about me. But she again said, with heavy emphasis, "Blame it on me. Just me. Tell the others." So I tried to spread her message around. Only next day did I understand her

18

gesture. When we met on the stairs Marylka, my one-time Guide captain and mentor, had been on her way to execution.

They then took me to the Castle, the Lublin prison, and I can still hear the sound of those heavy, wrought-iron, monumental gates clanging shut behind me. When I heard them clang to, I realised for the first time that I had lost my freedom. During interrogation at Gestapo headquarters (or 'under the clock' as we called it), I had been so busy concentrating on what I was saying that I gave no thought to what might lie ahead. But now I knew. There was no way out of this place. And only now did I begin to feel my body's pain – during the interrogations I had only been conscious of a childish delight in holding on and not betraying my friends; and in getting the better of my tormentors. I had even smiled throughout, no doubt enraging my captors still more.

Now I was at the Castle. Near me, all around the walls, were a number of men older than myself, and one younger man. I stood up with difficulty and slowly turned towards the boy. (We had all been ordered to stand facing the wall.) Immediately I received a fist in my face and felt the now familiar taste of blood. Like a small child, I burst into tears for the first time since I had been taken from my home – and I cried aloud for my mother. The man standing next to me shuddered and turned towards me, only to be knocked down by a blow from the guard. My chief tormentor who had just come in by a side door, mocked me in German: "Don't you worry. Your mother will be coming here too."

Suddenly that night they took me to a tiny cell crammed with women. When the door banged to, the women looked up from the bare planks on which they lay, two to each plank. These boards, pushed up close together, covered the whole area of the cell, except for a small space near the door where the latrine bucket stood. I stood helplessly in one corner, but none of the women spoke to me, though several turned and stared and one horribly bedraggled, half-naked hag inspected me from head to foot. "Bourgeoise," she spat accusingly.

19

They were filthy and stank so vilely that I went weak at the knees and keeled over on to the floor. I hit my head on the bucket, and that, oddly, brought me round. I sat down and a hideously dishevelled old woman screeched at me, "Get off the bucket, you whore." Obediently I stood up again and propped myself up against the door, my head pounding. I looked at those women, hoping to find one sympathetic face . . . One of them on the far side of the cell moved over and said: "Lie down." I took a look. Big white lice were crawling over the blanket. I drew back in horror, wanting to burst into tears again, but a mocking voice stopped me: "Is the little princess going to cry then?" I didn't cry, though I don't know how I managed not to, since I was crying in every fibre of my being. All through that first night I stayed in my corner near the door, even though one of the older women invited me to lie down. She spoke quietly and gently, and next morning I discovered she was a school-teacher and very kind. But that first night I was convinced that every one of them there was a murderess and a thief.

A few days after that they arrested Krysia. I knew her slightly, as she had been in the same Guide troop as myself, a pale, quiet girl, two years younger than me. Once, during the bombing in Lublin, the store room of St Adalbert's bookshop had caught fire, and the two of us had saved the books by carrying them to the cellar of the Capuchin Priory. I recognised Krysia at once and greeted her warmly, remembering only too well what my own first night in prison had been like.

Luckily, I was no longer alone among those women. A deep friendship was soon to spring up between myself and Krysia; and I was determined to protect her all I could.

2

If you have never seen a prison latrine, you will not be able to imagine it: two rows of holes in the ground, facing each other. Ten women – and a man standing at the end – it was too much for a young girl to cope with. That first week I suffered agonies, holding myself in, until bodily necessity overcame any feelings of shame. How could any human being ever forget such a shameful humiliation?

And in the prison itself we had to endure filthy conditions. There were lice, fleas and disease; as there was rarely any water, typhus broke out.

But, in spite of everything, we were young and healthy. Except for one thing: they had tied me up too tightly before beating me, and the rope had cut so deep into my flesh that an abscess had formed, a huge, painful suppuration. I could not sleep now, I had a raging temperature, and eventually they took me off to the prison hospital. The doctor looked at the abscess rather than at me and said:

"Mastitis. When did you give birth?"

"Give birth to what?"

Only then did he look at my face, and asked:

"Well, then, what *is* the matter with you?"

I didn't reply.

The abscess persisted for a long time. Then one day one of the women knocked into me accidentally and it burst. A sea of pus poured out, and the pain stopped. I still have the scar – the sole remaining witness to my interrogation by the Gestapo.

Shortly afterwards we were taken to an upstairs cell, a pleasant room which in fact belonged to the hospital: there had been so many arrests that the prison authorities had had to extend the women's section. The cell was light and clean, with a large window; and nearly all its occupants were 'politicals'. We breathed a sigh of relief.

We began to laugh again, to sing, to play bridge. Our parents did everything that was possible for us, bribing the guards to bring us some food. The first secret message from them was smuggled in inside a dumpling. At least our parents were still at home, and no one else from our families had been arrested. Every day we made playing-cards out of cardboard boxes in an effort to pass the time, and every day they took them away from us when the cell was searched.

Before long the cell became too small for the fifty-three women crowded into it. There was no room to lie down on the beds, and Krysia and I, as the two youngest, were made to sleep on a tiny, narrow table which was too small for any of the others. We developed our own way of sleeping, our 'two-snakes-devouring-each-other' technique; but even so, at first, the 'girls' had to strap us on to the table with a belt, so that we wouldn't fall off. We slept amazingly well on our bare table – when they let us.

Sometimes in the middle of the night, a light would suddenly snap on, we would be ordered to stand to attention, and our names and numbers read out. After that, of course, no one could get off to sleep again. We lay there, reciting prayers for the dying, since the inevitable sequence to such nocturnal visitations was a volley of shots just beneath our window, somewhere between the Castle and the outer wall.

Sometimes it happened every night, sometimes less often. One never knew when, or who . . . Now and again they shot their victims during the day.

On one such day, they did not call out our names but rounded up about half our cell including Krysia and myself. "At least we're together," sighed Krysia. Manicha began to recite the prayer 'Eternal rest, give unto us, O Lord'.

Before they led us away, I looked out of the window. Just above the bars a single branch of lilac was silhouetted against the sky. That white lilac was like a symbol of freedom, and it was flowering at the precise moment when we were being led out to our execution.

But – it was not death that awaited us. The prison commandant had simply decided that the conditions in our upstairs room were too pleasant, and that there were too many 'politicals' in the one place. So, we were being re-distributed among the other cells. Krysia and I were to be sent to Gencówna's.

Gencówna was the virtual 'queen' of the prison at that time. She was a beautiful prostitute who had initially come inside for the winter months, to leave again in summer. Eventually she came for good. In all probability she 'lived with' the authorities, and in general behaved as though she ruled the prison. She had a crowd of followers who catered for her every whim.

The 'queen' was kind to us, however, and seemed to like us. On her orders we were able to have a bath in the laundry where she herself bathed daily in a large tub. We were all right with Genca, and her cell, though dark and poky, was clean enough.

But we weren't left there for long. As a punishment for talking in the exercise yard, or something trivial like that, Krysia and I were cast down even lower, to the worst possible kind of cell in the bowels of the building. It was right by the reeking latrines and with room only for one, though in fact there were already three women sitting on the plank bed. One of these, a young, sixteen-year-old prostitute with terrifyingly pale eyes, aroused in me a sort of nameless dread. She had been arrested for murdering her child and had six fingers on each hand, six toes on each foot. I still find myself dreaming of those hideous white fingers.

Another prostitute in the cell was older, about twenty-five; but she looked fifty, she was ill and stank abominably. And there was only the one plank for all of us to lie on.

I don't know how I managed it, but somehow I persuaded Pogrebna, the normally very unpleasant man in charge of our section of the prison, to let us take the latrine door off its hinges and lay it on the cement floor for Krysia and me to sleep on. The stench was indescribably awful and bits of excrement floated round the floor.

We must have stirred Pogrebna's conscience because, after that, he allowed us to spend more time in the little prison yard. We hated having to return to the stinking cell, but we never voiced our feelings, not even to each other. Later we acquired another companion, one we could conjure up at will. Through clenched teeth we sang the old prison song of the Communists:

> Somewhere in a prison dungeon
> We shall become corpses.
> Instead of dying a little each day
> It's better that we should die together.
>
> Brothers, please believe me,
> It's far better to die than to live like this,
> spitting blood, blood, blood.
>
> We've strength enough and courage
> to gather the harvest of battle,
> either victorious laurels
> or a lingering hungry death.
>
> Comrades, we shall overcome,
> we shall never bow to force,
> spitting blood, blood, blood.
>
> For I have often known hunger,
> and hard times have been my lot.
> When they take me, I shall smile,
> – spit, swear, then die,
> spitting blood, blood, blood . . .

During the day, our prostitute companions were quite pleasant. One of them, Irka, known as 'the commander', was a charming girl of my own age. "You bourgeoisie don't know anything about life," she kept telling us. "You don't know how to live." Then she would tell us the most intimate details of her own existence, with such a lack of inhibition – she never 'worked' with older men, but always chose the younger ones – that Krysia could only stare at her open-mouthed. Irka, it transpired, was the daughter of a policeman who used to beat her as a punishment for her immoral behaviour. But it had made no difference. She loved her calling and said that we would never be able to understand.

In the end they took us out of that cell, though by that time we were old hands and had our own 'followers', who fashioned rings out of hair for us, while we made them rosaries out of bread. All the guards knew us and some of them had a soft spot for a quiet, pretty, graceful girl like Krysia. At one period, they even used to let us go into the loft, where we could watch people bringing parcels to the prison gate.

When Krysia and I first went up there the typhus epidemic was at its height. My first reaction was to draw back in panic: the floor was covered with a shiny, black, heaving sea of fleas. Never have I seen so many. We were instantly covered from head to foot with them. I looked round in horror – in one corner was a pile of corpses. Quickly I dragged Krysia round to the far side of the heap, out of range of the fleas. Fortunately she was not only innocent but also rather naive and credulous; there was much that escaped her notice. And as the years went by, there were many other things from which I managed to shield her.

After that we often went to the loft and even up to the tower, before our friendly guard was arrested and the visits abruptly ended. He once took us right to the top and gave us a couple of young rooks which had fallen out of the nest. For a time we went there secretly every day to feed the two birds, while all sorts of emotions welled up in our hearts: from that loft window I caught a glimpse of my father, standing there holding a parcel. His hair had gone quite grey.

3

As if lice, typhus and fleas were not enough, we were soon hit by a plague of scabies. It spread with incredible speed, as the filthy, overcrowded prison was an ideal breeding ground. In an attempt to keep the disease at bay, the Germans doused us with all sorts of evil-smelling liquids – but in vain.

It was not long before huge, festering swellings appeared on our aching, itching bodies. This wasn't ordinary scabies, but the 'horse' variety, distinguished by its septic sores and large, painfully inflamed swellings. We slept in such close proximity to each other that everyone would catch it. The disease came in various forms, but the Germans didn't worry about that, and treated all the symptoms in exactly the same way simply by pouring sulphuric acid over the infected areas. Septic sores, when doused with corrosive acid, festered even more and were very slow to heal. Krysia and I were both strong and healthy, and seemed to be astonishingly resistant since we had succumbed neither to the spotted fever nor to the typhus which took their toll of the prison, but our scabies cleared up only thanks to the ointments smuggled in to us from home.

Suddenly one day I was taken out of the cell and led downstairs. It was a beautiful spring day. At the gate stood an open car, and beside it my tormentor. I knew he had come for me.

Punctiliously he opened the car door and gestured to where I should sit. He himself got in the driver's seat and asked me where I would like to go. I stared at him. During my earlier interrogation – he had never once struck me himself, but always got others to do it – I had often thought that he was the handsomest man I had ever seen. Dark-complexioned, with jet black hair, dark eyes, a sharp, almost aquiline profile, and a scar over his upper lip. He was looking at me now quite strangely, and I didn't know what to make of it at all.

Once again he asked the question. I replied that, as he was driving, he presumably had some idea about where to go. He smiled, and the smile changed his face completely. "Wanda," he said, "be good to me, and I'll be good to you." I laughed nervously and forced myself to say quite casually: "Oh, I'm always good, I don't have it in me to be bad. I think I'd rather like to go to Sławinek." (My father and I often used to go for walks round there.)

Needless to say, I didn't believe he would take me up on it; Sławinek was several kilometres outside Lublin. But already he was cruising slowly through the town. The idea of escape flashed through my mind, and he must have read my thoughts for he smiled again, saying: "If you really are going to be good to me, you can't run away." In a state of rising terror, I was driven through the sunshine in that lovely car. At a crossroads, I caught sight of a teacher I knew, and her astonished and disbelieving face. I was about to wave to her when suddenly I became aware of my tormentor looking at me very oddly. I guessed that I was being shown to someone, or perhaps they were counting on me to point out someone to them. I glanced at the Gestapo man and nervously began to make polite conversation. He replied in kind and started telling me about his travels and about the years he had spent in China. He was lively and interesting on the subject. By now, we had left the town behind. Suddenly he stopped the car and got out. We sat in the sun, and I revelled in the beauty of the green meadows, the song of the birds and the sound of running water, while thinking of escape.

"I shouldn't try to run away, if I were you," he said again.

I didn't try. I knew I wouldn't stand a chance.

Then he drove me back. He returned me to the prison with as much formal politeness as if he had been escorting me to my own home. Once again there was the familiar clang of the gate, the stairs, the cell, the crowd of women. Excited questions greeted my arrival:

"What was the interrogation like?"

"Did they beat you?"

I swayed on my feet and Krysia ran to support me:

"What is it?"

"Nothing . . ."

They undressed me. I was neither bruised nor bleeding.

"What did they do to you?"

"Where did they take you?"

"Slawinek," I said truthfully.

For a moment they stared at me as though I were mad, and then silence fell over the entire cell. All of them, except Krysia and Władka, drew away from me.

"Spy!" one of them spat.

"It's obvious she's his lover," said another.

I said nothing . . . I had lost confidence in those women, I resented them bitterly, for they had caused me even more suffering than had the Gestapo.

Once again I was close to tears and desperately tired. Later that night, when the others were asleep, I told Krysia what had happened. In fact, nothing had happened, yet for many nights after that I was unable to sleep for wondering what it had all really meant. I still wonder why he took me to Sławinek.

The women continued to treat me suspiciously for quite a long time. I didn't really blame them, but their attitude hurt. I had learned one thing: never again would I return a straightforward, honest answer, as I had that night. From then on, I confided only in Krysia and Władka. And perhaps it was then that I stopped being a child.

4

The prison days dragged slowly by. We were exhausted by the endless inactivity punctuated by bouts of punishment; and by the daily pitiless summons to execution, for which we all waited our turn. The prisoners fell into two very different categories: the 'politicals' – and the criminals, who were our deadly enemies. It was the latter who often made our lives a misery.

Suddenly, from out of the blue, came the news that some prisoners were to be transported to a concentration camp.

A group of prisoners under sentence was taken out by a prison guard to work in the fields. To this day I don't know how our parents managed to persuade this guard to include us in their number, but one day we were marched off along the street in rows of five, our legs fairly buckling with exhaustion. When we got to the field, there were all our nearest and dearest. Oh, God, it was a nightmare. If our families had only known what that meeting would cost us, I think they would not have tried to arrange it. I don't know how we kept from weeping. We couldn't try to escape, of course, because our guard, who trusted our families, would have paid for it with his life. Returning to the prison with our loved ones, not daring to speak, was even harder to bear than any interrogation by the Gestapo. A storm of longing burst over us, and I think that that was the first time I asked myself the question, 'Why should this happen to me?'

I don't know what my parents' thoughts were, as they walked behind us on the pavement, and I resented them dragging me out of prison just so that they could have a glimpse of me . . . Could they not understand what it meant to have to return there again? I wanted to run away, to dash up the first street we passed. They'd shoot me, and there would be an end. But I hated the thought of going back. God, how I longed to be free! I marked a particular street-corner, and decided to make a dash for it. At that moment Krysia reached out for my hand, though she could not have guessed my thoughts. No one knew about my moment of rebellion . . . and I forced my thoughts away from it.

Of course, they wouldn't have shot just me, but the man who had trusted my mother, and almost certainly my mother too. Outwardly calm, I returned to the prison, though my legs felt like cotton-wool, and I was very, very tired.

We were all exhausted after that excursion. It was as though we had been put through an interrogation. Our families had given us the news that we were to be transported to a concentration camp, though I have no idea how they had come by the information.

The news didn't scare us at all. Our knowledge of the camps was vague in the extreme, and in fact the word 'camp' had pleasant associations for us, calling to mind the joyous sunlit settings for our Girl Guide gatherings. There was nothing in my previous experience of that word which could possibly have evoked terror.

Besides, we were utterly fed up with prison. Those ghastly, overcrowded cells, the hordes of endlessly squabbling women who bit and scratched when they ran out of words: it was all so dreadful that it seemed impossible to us that anywhere else could actually be worse. Filth, lice, enforced idleness, constant harassment, endless searches, the long nights waiting for death – it was more than we could bear.

One night they came and woke Mrs Śniegocka – a lovely woman, with velvet brown eyes and a gentle face. She put on a light brown dress with a finely pleated skirt, and went off to her execution that night, talking about her daughter who was about our age. We were deeply affected by her death.

I can't write the names of all those who passed through that prison, those who came out and those who did not.

The youngest and most militant of us formed a secret group; we called ourselves the black tablers. It was really no more than a gesture of defiance.

On 21 September a list of prisoners who were 'to go in the transport' was read out in the prison yard. Ever since the previous afternoon we had known that something was in the air. When our names were read out, we sighed with relief; we all thought we had been summoned for immediate execution. Being sent off to a camp was unexpected, and even though the names of those who had already been sentenced to death appeared on the list, we felt sure that the camp somehow spelled a reprieve. How naive we were! We did not know that, even after years in the camp, we could still be gassed or shot. Standing in that prison yard we believed that executions were carried out only there – over in that blind alley between the walls . . .

It was a bright, cheerful September day. So many of the terrible things I have seen have happened on beautiful sunny September days . . .

This particular one was glorious, shimmering with heat, but we struggled with conflicting emotions. We were relieved that only the 'politicals' were leaving, that the prostitutes who ruled over the Castle were staying behind. After those terrible prison days, any change seemed likely to be for the better. Only later did life show us that every change was always change for the worse. That was how it was to be during the endless days, months and years which lay ahead. But not until much later did we discern the pattern.

I looked round at those familiar faces, some of them now so dear to me – and felt a sudden fear. What if they arranged us in alphabetical order? . . . Krysia, where are you? Well, no matter where she was, we would be together in spirit. No one could prevent that. Apart from one moment when I believed I was on the way to my death, I always wanted her by my side.

When the list had been checked, we could choose where to 'stand'. Our 'black tablers' grouped together in the men's courtyard, because there was more room there than

31

in the women's yard. We stood there the whole day. We could not see anyone, but we knew that through every crack in the boarded-up windows, a thousand anxious eyes were watching us. There were several women among us who had been arrested along with their husbands, and for some of the male prisoners it was probably the last time they would ever see their wives.

This was to be the first large women's transport to a concentration camp. Transport number 154, destination unknown . . . Oh, the human imagination is without limits, and often soars beyond the frontiers of reason. A thousand rumours ran through the yard; the rows of women were alive with excited speculation. We were going – to work, to the Tyrol, to Bavaria, to . . . to . . . to . . . Honestly, I was surprised no one said we were going to London, since everything seemed possible.

We stood there, hot and sweaty, wearing all the clothes we possessed. It might be cold where we were going, we might be hungry, perhaps we could sell our meagre possessions for food. In fact the prison commandant, Dominik, a blond giant of a man who was generally agreed to be 'not such a bad fellow', had made an announcement: "Women, you don't need to take anything with you. They'll give you whatever you need. You'll be better off there." But we didn't believe him. We knew we could never believe anything they told us. So we stood there, picturesque as market women in their thirteen petticoats, looking as wide as we were high. Some of us were wearing curlers, some had made up their faces carefully, thinking that perhaps it might be for the last time . . . I looked up and saw the old castle dungeons outlined against the sky. Seven months of imprisonment behind me – days which I remembered only with dread, which I wanted above all to forget.

Emotions raged within us. How often were we torn apart by conflicting emotions, being absolutely sure one minute that our luck would hold, that justice would finally triumph; and at the next, burning with helpless desires and sinking into a black trough of depression about the future, into that worst of all fears, the terror of the unknown.

"Women, here's some sausage. You'll see, it'll be better where you're going," booms the voice of the huge German.

Better?

Towards evening, the trucks arrive, and we get in. Somehow, right from the beginning it turned out that I was in a group of women who considered themselves 'responsible' for the rest. So we let everyone else go first, and we brought up the rear. We wanted to be together, we were all we had . . .

I held on to Krysia's hand. From the surgery window a despairing hand waved. I didn't know who it was, and it didn't really matter. Quite suddenly I was overwhelmed by the absolute certainty of terrible things to come. I was suspended in a void, without landmarks, without any visible means of support.

"We've got to hold on, we've got to, do you hear?" I shouted to Krysia over the roar of the truck's engine. "We've got to come back."

And with that we went away. Once again the gate clanged shut behind us. This time we were on the other side.

5

We went out via the town centre, through the streets we knew so well. Through a slit in the canvas, we spotted the familiar face of a friend, Danuta. It was getting dark and I couldn't even make out her eyes, but I knew they were blue. They loaded us into the passenger wagons, about eight to each compartment. What luxury! The train stood in the station for a long time. Night fell, a silent, starry night, warm and full of mystery. Do you remember, Joanna? You sat on a step and told us the story of a magic island . . . We listened to you in silence, each of us lost in her own thoughts and dreams. I remember my own thoughts very well. I wanted to run away, but I was afraid they would arrest my mother if I did so. There were many women languishing in Lublin Castle because of their connection with somebody else . . . No, that was out of the question, at least for the present . . . Perhaps, later on, wherever it was we were going, where our families would not be held responsible for whatever we did.

Responsible. A powerful word . . . That night, I felt responsible for ensuring that Krysia should one day return home. I don't really know why. But I determined then, as I was to do so often in future years, that she, at least, *must* return. Little Krysia, only seventeen . . . I looked at her . . . She was asleep, the train rocking her like a child.

The wheels seemed to say: back-we'll-come-back-we'll-come-back . . .

Next day dawned clear and bright. The Polish autumn was bidding us goodbye with a golden smile – and on a day which was vibrant with a thousand colours. At one station a small boy threw a bunch of flowering heather to us, a handful of lilac-coloured twigs which smelled of the earth. Never had I known heather to smell so sweet; they were the first flowers we had held in our hands for over seven months.

There were prisoners from Pawiak in the carriages behind us, and that long train, as it pursued its way, carried on board hundreds of hearts that quivered with pain. I won't cry, I told myself. Not until I am home again. I won't cry until I can fling myself down in the long grass and look up at the sky, at the waving branches silhouetted against it. I won't cry. I won't. – And I didn't. None of us did.

Someone threw a letter out of the window. "We are heading into the unknown, via Kutno and Poznań." (The letter was found and delivered.)

To-the-unknown-to-the-unknown-to-the-unknown . . . sang the wheels in rhythm.

Frightened faces at the station. Everyone knew the misery contained in those wagons surrounded by SS guards. "A train-load of women going into exile," someone said. Exile? Oh, yes, that much was sure, but only now did we have to face the question head on. Where, exactly, were they sending us? To-the-unknown-to-the-unknown . . .

Poznań. Suddenly we had left Poland behind. For how long? Perhaps for ever. "Dear God, let me die in Poland," Staszka cried out loud. Die? No, no, we didn't want to die, not even on Polish soil. And if we had to, did it really matter where? Oh yes, it mattered. Something deep inside us insisted that it mattered a great deal.

The second night of the journey was even worse than the first. In the course of it, we passed through Berlin. Darkness. Blackout. Early on the morning of 23 September 1941 we read the name 'Fürstenberg' – a new, meaningless place. A name which conveyed nothing, a shapeless name without memories. Yet, today? What does that name arouse in you today, Wanda? Will you ever be able to utter it without fear? Will it always, to the end of your life, drench you with dread? Even then we shuddered . . . it was cold – we were hungry and desperately tired from our two sleepless nights.

They arranged us in rows of five, and that was our first glimpse of the women overseers; our new masters. There are no words to describe the vileness of those women. They looked at us with contempt, those crow-women in their black hooded capes, those raven-women, as we came to call them. Enormously tall, blonde giantesses, with hard, empty eyes, tightly compressed lips and harsh, strident voices, they were always accompanied by huge wolfhounds as if their presence wasn't threatening enough.

We stood motionless and silent, surrounded by that pack of fierce dogs and those hostile, inhuman humans. Brutal voices and gestures, kicks, blows, slaps – immediately, from the very first moment, a leaden fear clutched at our hearts. I stood there, clenching my teeth so hard that my jaws ached. That's what I remember most clearly – my jaws aching from the bite of despair. We stayed silent, beginning to suspect what was in store for us over the next days or even months. It did not enter our heads that we should have been counting in years.

Silence . . . ominous silence . . .

Later we would often experience the horror of such mass silence; but that first time was the worst. It was so unexpected, so shattering, so new, so pregnant with panic fear – the first silence which had ever filled us with shame. With sudden clarity I looked round at my friends; their faces seemed somehow different. The same, yet unrecognisable: ashen masks, eyes stubbornly fixed on the ground. Why were we avoiding each other's gaze? Why did I not lash out at those hideous women with my bare fists the first time they struck one of us across the face? But we were all overwhelmed with shame in the face of our own terror, our utter helplessness, our humiliation, and the sheer physical weakness which plagued us.

We continued to stand there in our rows, waiting for transport; despised female convicts, human flotsam cast out of life's mainstream.

Even the awareness that we were all together no longer afforded us much consolation. On the contrary, it made the pain of humiliation more unbearable. Suddenly I experienced a moment of raging hatred: what the hell, I'll go for that one nearest me and hang the consequences. I tensed myself, getting ready to spring. The black cape came nearer . . . if she strikes Krysia or Władka or me, I'll . . . I looked her straight in the eye . . . She averted her gaze, passed on and that time round did not hit any of us. Slowly I unclenched my jaws. God, how they hurt!

We were taken to the camp in trucks. At a crossroads we could see the sparkling waters of a lake, and high above it a forest which seemed almost to float in the sky. The camp was immediately below the forest: from the walls we could see that ethereal landscape outlined against the sky, and its very nearness increased the pain of our separation. How I longed for that forest . . . and, oh, the times without number I dreamed of it.

Throughout those days without hope, the forest remained my symbol of freedom, of peace and repose. Even now, whenever I feel troubled, I want to run to the forest first, and only afterwards do I turn to people for help.

RAVENSBRÜCK. The show camp. A gate and a large square – a few buildings in the foreground, and on the other side of the square, on both sides of the camp's main street, rows of identical low barracks. Square and street alike strewn with cinders. Rows of salvias in flower, their flamboyant scarlet in some way symbolic. Innocent flowers which I shall hate forever.

We looked round curiously. A smooth, high wall, far too high for any escape. Over it, electrified wires and watch-towers. We could tell even from this first encounter that it was a closely guarded, sealed camp.

In the distance I saw women walking in rows of five, all identically dressed in blue-grey striped uniforms. We all looked at them with avid curiosity. What struck me was the terrifying blank sameness of their faces, quite indistinguishable each from the other.

It was then I understood that here was something infinitely worse than the filth of the prison – those clean, identically shaved heads, those lifeless, expressionless faces. They walked past with indifference, not looking at us, not speaking, not reacting to our presence in any way. They did not seem to have faces. They are nothing but husks, I thought. And there, on that square, a silent prayer was wrenched from me: "Oh God, if you still have a care for your world, grant that we may keep our own faces in this dreadful place. Never mind our lives, but do not let our spirits die . . ."

Numbers . . . numbers . . . numbers. Nothing else. No surnames . . . no given names . . . no feeling. "Those women are already dead," I thought. Krysia grasped my hand: "They all look exactly alike," she said in a terrified whisper. Realising that she was panic-stricken at the sight I spoke hastily: "Well, you know, it's the shaven heads that give that impression." She sighed with relief, but it was cold comfort: I knew that we were both afraid of it happening to us.

Yet not everybody passed us by without a word. There were still some 'living' Polish women, the ones with red triangles on their striped shifts (we hadn't yet learned that red denoted a political prisoner). As they passed by, they sneaked a smile at us, urging us to throw our bits and pieces to the ground so that they might pick them up. "Sondertransport" they all whispered to us, using the German word. We didn't know what they meant, nor why they should so designate us. Only long afterwards did we discover that a Special Transport was a transport of women who had been condemned to death. To put it bluntly, we were to be exterminated, some of us immediately, others later on.*

But on that day, 23 September 1941, we were still

* It later emerged that we had indeed all been sentenced to death – without trial, without a prosecution and without any possibility of defence. The Lublin Gestapo were renowned for the extreme penalties they imposed, regardless of either guilt or the age of the offender!

unaware of the sentence, and there was nothing remarkable or special about the way our transport was treated. Like everyone else, we were taken to the bath house and stood in line waiting our turn. There were a lot of young girls in our transport, especially Girl Guides (the youngest was only fifteen) and most of us were well-educated; what the Lublin prostitutes had called 'those damned politicals'. The majority of our group had been arrested for some resistance activity we had undertaken voluntarily. I looked at the lines of women, who would within minutes be stripped of their civilian clothing. They were tense and wary. Watching them, I wondered how many of us would come through, how many of today's arrivals would be able to preserve her own 'face'.

Quarantine . . .

The long days went by, indistinguishable one from another, stupefying in their bleak hopelessness. The Germans were terrified of infection and prisoners in quarantine were kept in the strictest isolation. Crammed into a dining hall, we waited in enforced silence, from one meal, one roll-call, to the next. Nothing but waiting, endless waiting.

Each morning, we would wake to the wail of the siren and begin on the nightmare of bed-making. Seven bunks high, thirty-five across, and only eighteen pillows. I shudder when I think of all the hours we wasted making 'hospital corners', all the blind rage which had to be swallowed when, for the umpteenth time, Hermina, our brisk, German block-leader, dismantled the beds we had just made with so much difficulty. She nagged and bullied – we could never do anything right: an overall incorrectly buttoned-up, a dirty glass, a grubby pocket and a thousand excuses for bringing it home to us that this was a camp, and that punishment was all we could expect from it. Oh yes, Hermina was great at handing out punishments and stuffing our heads full of camp regulations, familiarising us with words like Rewir (camp hospital), Punishment Block, and Bunker. And we, a passive lumpen mass, were reduced to submission from the word go. What was the

39

matter with us? We were disorientated, we had lost our sense of identity. That mass of women . . . It seemed so impossibly overcrowded to us then; and yet, before the camp had finished with us, there would be five times our present number crowded into a barracks of equal size. To us it was all so new and alien: that senseless hurry, the wire mesh that separated us from the camp proper.

One day we were all given a number, and after that we ceased to exist as our former selves. A number on a striped sleeve, that's all we were. "My people," Hermina called us.

Then they let us send our first postcard home. Number and address, plus the information that we were in 'Ravensbrück-in-Mecklenburg Women's Concentration Camp'. That was all.

It was tough. But we did not know that it was only a beginning. With the optimism of youth, we convinced ourselves that over there, in the camp itself, things would be better. Bored with inactivity, we were itching to be put to work. It's hard to believe we could have been so naive!

Quite soon after that they split us up between two blocks, 13 and 15. We were quite accustomed to the stripes by now and no longer burst out laughing at the sight of a shaven head. We were learning the language of the camp, from Hermina and some of the older camp inmates who secretly came to talk to us.

These 'veterans' taught us how to avoid a bad report, since that would mean being arrested and sentenced to death by slow starvation in the Bunker. They warned us against ever falling ill, since admission to the rewir meant being kicked or beaten to death. They taught us how to distinguish between the actions which would send us to the punishment block and those which merited only a cut in the coffee ration.

While still on the wrong side of the fence we had become haunted by the sight of the 'Goldstücks' (pieces of gold) – the name we gave to those wretched women who had been dehumanised by the hateful life of the camp. A Goldstück was a woman who devoured anything she could find, even garbage like rotten potato peelings; a woman who stole from her companions; a woman who was no more than a vegetable. The thought that the camp might stifle our humanity, crush us, destroy us as individuals, was an unspeakable torment.

The women we had glimpsed behind the wire were like brute beasts, and we dreaded becoming like them. We wanted to survive, but not like that; it was imperative to stay as we were, normal women, strong and full of life. We were terrified of what we might become. And so aided perhaps by instinct we began, quite consciously, to erect defences round our essential humanity, to protect ourselves against becoming brutalised, to keep scrupulously clean.

Right from the start we set about organising some kind of cultural life for ourselves. It was difficult and dangerous, but it was the only way we could hope to triumph over the prison stripes. Stories, lectures, recitations, solo and choral singing, sketches, riddles, poetry. We took a lot of time and trouble over such activities. Our block leader in number 15, big, fat Hermina – who lost no opportunity of screaming and nagging at us – occasionally relented enough to listen to our efforts, though our attempts at singing usually drove her mad.

We used to sing favourite songs from our earlier prison repertoire, light-hearted pieces, some of them sentimental, like 'A Little Street In Barcelona' or 'Faithful River'; battle songs, soldiers' songs, scouting songs. We were very soon putting our own words to the old tunes, and soloists would volunteer to sing them at our concerts and musical evenings. Pola and Stenia would sing, Joanna too, though her real speciality was reciting verse. Giga went in for humorous monologues and Grażyna composed poems which she read out to us.

Beneath our windows, tall golden sunflowers defied the bleak greyness of the blocks. When it rained or the wind blew, one of them would tap its head against the window. Grażyna's favourite sunflower not only tapped but looked in at us and teased us with its bright, laughing face. Grażyna wrote a poem about it.

I can't remember the words of the poem, and Grażyna is long dead, shot in the camp. But her poem outlived her, that poem about the sunflower which brought a solitary gleam of splendour into our grey quarantine. It was a poem filled with longing – and by that time we were a single scream of longing; during those weeks of quarantine we were on fire with life, and longing seethed within us, mingling with a host of other emotions.

Roll-calls were our salvation, for at those times we could watch magnificent sunrises and sunsets when the sky was radiant with unimaginable colours. The sky was not our enemy, it was wonderful, it healed us, allowed us to escape in imagination, to forget. Fierce winds whipped up seas of brightly-coloured clouds, turning them before our eyes into fantastic shapes, of dragons and knights and scenes from the story-books.

Then our quarantine came to an end.

It had seemed so endless that today I can scarcely believe that it lasted for only six weeks. We were chafing at the forced inactivity which seemed only to underline our total helplessness. So we waited impatiently for it to end, deluding ourselves that any change must be for the better. In spite of the lessons we had already learned in prison, it was a long time before we shed that particular illusion.

Then, everything changed.

Up to that time, in the quarantine block, we had only attended head-count roll-calls which checked up on the number of prisoners in the camp. These head-counts took place twice every day, morning and evening for varying lengths of time, sometimes for hours on end. The register had to tally, that is to say that the number of women present had to match the number on the official list. As the camp population was very fluid, and new groups of prisoners were always arriving, counting very often took an inordinately long time. As new arrivals we found ourselves placed in the worst positions and subjected to the most unpleasant experiences. Unlike the older inmates of the camp, we were not assigned to regular work units, but formed the 'labour pool' and could be selected for anything at all.

The system of work was as follows: apart from essential duties in the blocks, such as sewing and mending, there was also a lot of manual labour required within the camp compound: carrying briquettes of fuel to the furnaces, carting stones and bricks on barrows, unloading boats, digging ditches and so forth. No special work-units were assigned to these various manual jobs, but a unit leader or overseer, usually a German woman, would select prisoners for their work-parties during the labour roll-call.

Fresh from quarantine, we as yet knew little about the camp hierarchy; nor did we know anything about the different kinds of labour for which we were selected. Our block-leader, the zealous Hermina, regarded it as a point of honour to 'sell' us all at the labour calls; and she managed to find the very nastiest jobs for us to do. In those early days we worked very hard, probably too hard, and performed the sort of tasks which nowadays I would think quite impossible for young women to do. Especially young women who were hungry.

We soon changed our minds about inactivity being the worst of all evils, and after long days of hard physical toil we found ourselves dreaming of idleness. We had no notion of malingering, but put our whole selves into our work, having not yet learned that it was the ones who managed to shirk, to avoid the worst tasks while making a show of working hard, who were most likely to survive. How could we have known? We carried monstrous loads on our backs, in our arms or on barrows; and in the evenings we fell on our beds in a stupor. We ached all over, as all those long-unused muscles took their revenge. Poor 'new girls', harassed by the heavy boots of the SS, and by the scorn of the more cunning older inhabitants, we had soon become little more than beasts of burden.

Occasionally Krysia and I would be picked for an un-familiar work-team, which perhaps sounded less arduous than the others. For example, one day they sent us to 'the gardens'. But on arrival we found the 'gardening' to consist of carrying stones from the lake-shore up the hill to the overseers' homes. The gardens of the SS were surrounded by harmless-looking stone walls. But they were made of stones that we had to carry in our arms or push in wheelbarrows up the hill; and the terrain was laid out in such a way that our barrows were always full on the upward journey.

But even this, as it later turned out, was not the worst job of all. The greatest nightmare hid behind an innocent-sounding word, the sand job.

When we first heard it, we inevitably associated sand with beaches and river-banks, with sunlight and summer. But this sand turned out to be pure torture. It was work specially invented for those 'new girls' who had not been selected during the morning's labour call. In a show camp like Ravensbrück, all prisoners had to work, and if there was not enough work to go round, then hundreds of women were simply given spades and put to shifting mounds of sand all day long. Each woman had a mound to shift. There was a whole chain of mounds, and no shortage of sand, since the woman next to you simply shifted her sand on to your pile all day long. And she did so with all the strength at her command, because a camp overseer with a dog stood over her shouting, "Faster, faster, come on, get a move on." The spades blistered the palms of our hands, and the sand, heavy and damp in the morning, would, as the day wore on, be whipped by the fierce Mecklenburg winds into fine, shifting grains which choked our eyes, ears and mouths, and penetrated through our clothing. We returned home smothered in sand. We felt as though it were burying us alive.

Tried out on many hundreds of women, it was unfailingly successful. The sand swamped many of us. It was the last straw which put an end to our initiative, and saw off our literary evenings. If I did not want to avoid pathos, I would say that that sand smothered our very spirits – and turned us into little more than husks.

The blisters on our hands hardened into callouses, and

we grew used to wielding spades. But our colour faded as each day passed, and our striped dresses hung from us ever more loosely. We were losing weight rapidly now, and our legs and necks were becoming scrawnier and scraggier. We were hungry, always hungry, and hunger prevented us from sleeping.

Yet, every so often, as we shuffled those idiotic piles in the full realisation that what we did was totally devoid of meaning, we would find ourselves wanting to rebel. Sometimes there was the aching desire to run away over the sand. But then hopelessness would take over. Rebellion? What could we do in our position? Better to become as numb and unfeeling as the stones. For if we continued to entertain such feelings and desires, we would go mad. Far better to settle for being a 'husk'.

So we became greyer and uglier; and our smiles came less and less often.

Time passed, the days grew shorter – frost and snow – winter . . . November, December 1941. In our sleeping-quarters icicles hung from the rafters, the blankets became covered with hoar frost, and Hermina would systematically order all the windows on both sides of the room to be opened. We thought we would die of cold that winter. But we didn't even get ill, didn't catch so much as a cold. In spite of everything, we hung on to life. In coats that contained not a single shred of wool and which were full of holes, we stood for hours in the frost, and a malign fate continued to keep us alive. But sometimes in the evening before sleep, we would give way to self-pity. My bones ached so dreadfully, was it possible we had once been human? Had we ever really lived another kind of life? Could sand, the golden sand on the Vistula River, for example, once have seemed a symbol of freedom? And did the forests still rustle?

Out of self-protection, we told each other stories. Do you remember, Krysia, the fantastic tales I used to spin for you, as you did for me? I don't remember them now, but I know that some were simply about walks in the mountains. You told me about the paths you knew, and we promised each other that one day we would walk them together.

6 December 1941. The present. They held an extra roll-call and divided us into three groups. We were afraid they would separate us, but they didn't. We were still together. They put us in three work detachments, and we began the first night-shift. At first it seemed as though work inside the barracks would at least be a change for the better, and we even smiled as we set off that first night, even though they were driving us along with whips.

The barrack-room was long and dirty. Our job was to select straw and plait it to make boots for the guards. The din was deafening, the atmosphere stifling . . . They had sent us to a barracks where there were no other Polish women at all, only strange, ugly, repulsive crones with expressions that I didn't understand at the time, but which I later came to fear: rank-smelling gypsies and some old German women with whom we had almost nothing in common.

The air was so thick with dust that I could scarcely breathe. I stood next to a gypsy woman and began to plait the straw braids; the damp straw immediately cut into my hands and made them bleed. I don't know how I kept going until five the next morning, but I did. After that there was a change of shift and they threw us out, sweating and exhausted, into the frosty air wearing only our thin, short-sleeved summer dresses. We had been given those dresses for work, since it was so hot in the barracks; and we had to wear them all the time. In those thin, inadequate garments we stood for hours at roll-call. We made sick jokes about them to cheer ourselves up, but our own particular 'black crow' would fly into a rage when a sudden burst of laughter came from our ranks.

Those night roll-calls, necessitated by our new hours of work, had a kind of fascination which in spite of everything was undeniable. I remember one night when we stood under a sky full of stars: a dark blue sky, two lanterns and our own shadows . . . I don't know who it was – Bogna, perhaps, who suggested that our row of worn-out skeletons would fit well into a horror movie. We had ridiculous caps on our heads, which cast grotesque shadows on the snow as we swayed about. At Bogna's suggestion, we tried out different effects for our hypothetical film, moving our heads from side to side, while the shadows danced with grotesque grace across the snow.

Our 'crow' (these days we reserved the name for her alone, whereas at first we had applied it to all our overseers) was dark, with a huge mane of tousled hair and a cheap permanent wave. Her voice was shrill and piercing, and she was something of a sadist. She was excessively pernickety and was hell to work for. Of all those who supervised our work with the plaited straw, she was by far the worst. She loathed it when we laughed, and so we laughed more often when she was around than at any other time. Maybe that tiny bit of defiance which that horrible woman aroused in us made us feel that we were still human.

But by and large things had gone from bad to worse. Time passed without news of the outside world, and with no hope for an end to the war or even the slightest improvement of our lot. We were abandoned, forgotten ciphers, human beings on the margin of life.

The pace increased. First there was hunger; then hunger plus heavy manual labour; then hunger, hard labour and restless nights. We were reduced to an urgent longing for sleep, sleep, sleep. We even fell asleep on our feet at roll-call, with our eyes still wide-open. Sometimes we fell down. We used to slap each other on the back to get warm, so that we would not fall on to the frosty ground. We called it 'American massage' – don't ask me why. Short, sharp slaps delivered in rapid succession with the flat of the hand. It helped. It warmed the one who did the slapping as much as the one who was slapped.

Or we would stamp our feet on the frosty gound, singing Bogna's song under our breath. In fact we no longer called her Bogna, but had re-christened her 'long Jim' because she had become very skinny and lanky, and her favourite song was a negro foxtrot about a black cotton-picker called Jim. We knew all the words, but of course were forbidden either to sing or to stamp our feet, so we ran the risk of being brutally kicked by the 'crow'. But in those days of utter hopelessness, we had to look for our salvation wherever we might find it.

6

Days . . .

Yes, you *could* reckon the experience in days, but the sum of those days would tell you nothing. It was difficult to survive even one twenty-four-hour span. Days in the camp could not be measured against any normal yardstick; no one outside our world could begin to imagine just how long a single day could be in such a place. You could indeed say that every day lasted an eternity. It was an unimaginable nightmare.

And so we went on. With no day of rest, no break, every day and every night, straw . . . straw . . . straw . . . stench, an ever-accelerating tempo, and the voice that goaded without cease: "Get a move on, faster, faster!"

Our hands and fingers became so swollen that we could not put our hands together. After the night-shift we would return to the block at five in the morning, sleep for an hour, then stand interminably at roll-call, aching with exhaustion, unbearably tired, before returning to the block. It was so cold in our bunks that it was hours before we could catch sleep, and when at last we drifted off, the camp siren would waken us for yet another roll-call. Only after the midday meal (warmed-up watery soup or swedes) were we free to sleep till four, when the counting started again. And even during those few precious hours intended for sleep, Hermina often dropped in on us, screaming at full throttle.

Our first Christmas in the camp. I remember it so well! Winter was especially cruel to us that year, with howling gales and sharp frosts, and Christmas Eve exactly like any other day. It brought no let-up from the choking straw, nor from the rowdiness of our gypsy, fellow-workers.

The overseer that night was a 'good' one, and she allowed

each group to sing a national carol. The Germans sang first, though 'Silent Night' sounded strangely ill-suited to those noisy surroundings. We Poles at first didn't want to join in, but then we changed our minds. Why not sing a Polish carol and hear it wing its way far into the night sky? But when we came to the words, 'Take my hand, O Christ Child', we choked on our tears and could not continue. We felt ashamed of those tears, but who could have blamed us for shedding them?

We always tried to avoid tears. I scarcely ever cried (three, maybe four times in all), but on that occasion, darkness swam before my eyes. The women's voices sounded different; softer than usual and more tender. In our mind's eye we all pictured the familiar images of home: the Christmas wafer . . . the Christmas tree . . . well-loved faces . . . the church organ . . . the church itself at midnight mass. What were our loved ones doing that night? Were there really people, somewhere in the world, who were gathering peacefully round a green fir tree in love and celebration?

Getting through that day – or, rather, that Vigil night – was painful. On our return to the block, we broke down completely and cried our hearts out. It was Władka's and Joanna's fault. On the table they had placed a tiny Christmas tree – where they had obtained it was their secret – and on the tree were little toys which Joanna had roughly carved out of toothbrush handles: miniature elephants with their trunks held high as a sign of joy; tiny boats; hearts . . . Later on, she would do more elegant carvings, but these first efforts of hers were the most moving of all – reminders, along with our little Polish Christmas tree, of our lost freedom.

We felt terribly sad, and yet somehow that day we regained our identity. Once again we discovered the hope that, after all, we were still living, breathing, sentient human beings and suddenly we felt very close and peaceful in each other's company.

And so Christmas passed without any more tears being shed, though they were always just below the surface.

Perhaps to taunt us, the Germans had put up a tree in the camp street: a tree with fairy lights, which we walked past each day, weary with our duties. We showed a calm, unruffled face to the world, but inside we were a mass of pain and longing. Don't cry, girl. For God's sake, don't cry.

And with that first Christmas in the camp the year 1941 came to an end.

Long, dreary days passed, and a new temptation came to confront us: to satisfy our hunger at any cost. The struggle against hunger – the struggle to persuade a starving stomach not to think about food – sapped what was left of our strength. We believed in the beginning that where there was a will, there was a way, and that those who fell by the wayside had just not tried hard enough. But how could we acquire such will-power – I *will* do it. I will – which was a witness to our inner freedom. And how were we going to hang on to it? In mute answer our emaciated frames throbbed with a single resolve: "As long as I can exercise my will, I am free; as long as I can exercise my will, I shall not steal. I am still *me*." Thus was our physical torment matched by an impossible mental anguish. It was intolerable to be so constrained.

I shall never know how we managed to survive the physical labour: straw-plaiting, however unpleasant, was soon superseded by even more terrible tasks, and we were beginning to grasp the one sacred law of the camp – that any change would always, infallibly, be for the worse. On one occasion I was forced to carry eighty kilos of cement on my back up two flights of narrow stairs to a loft. I managed it only because another prisoner was right behind me, and if I had fallen on her with that load I would have killed her. I simply had no alternative, so I kept going.

In February 1942 came an apparent respite: the demand for work suddenly slumped. But it meant, of course, that they had to invent more of their highly unpleasant jobs for us to do. Krysia and I were sent back to 'gardening' duties; pushing barrow-loads of earth and stones, digging trenches in ground that was frozen hard. Sometimes we had to cart snow. You can't imagine how heavy a barrow-load of white, feathery snow can be when the barrow-pushers are weak and starving women. The barrows we used had been standing half-submerged at the edge of the lake, and they were so heavy and waterlogged that Krysia could barely move them. From the lakeside the road wound uphill to the overseers' houses. At the top of the hill was a forest, and beyond the forest a pitiless sky. Sodden wheelbarrows, and we had to cart all that snow to the top of the hill in them. Full on the way up, empty coming down. You couldn't do it, Krysia, the barrow kept running away from you. I tied your hands to the barrow so that they wouldn't slip, because, if they had, there was a purpose-trained dog standing by, waiting for the chance to fly at you. I walked behind you, and I couldn't see that you were crying, until I reached the top and saw the barrow fall from your hands and your little face drenched in tears. I ran to you, and persuaded you to stay at the top, while I went back down below for more snow. I turned round more smartly than usual so that the overseer wouldn't notice anything; and Krysia took hold of the wheelbarrow again, just in time. Our scheme worked for a while, but then one of them spotted us. She fell on Krysia with a horsewhip, shrieking: "What's the matter with you?" The dog, a huge wolf-hound, snarled and bared its teeth. I could stand no more. Flinging myself between the whip and Krysia, I seized the whip in my hand and shouted at the woman: "Can't you see that the child is all in?" She turned to face me, with an expression of utter astonishment on her face. But she didn't strike either of us. She just bent down to lace up her riding boots, then strode off. For the rest of the day she kept her distance, and Krysia stayed at the top of the hill. I felt quite cheerful: "Where there's a will," I thought, "even here there may be a way . . ."

We carried sacks of all sizes, bags, blocks of compressed fuel, and God knows what else. It was all much too heavy for us and we were at the end of our strength. Or at least, that was what we thought then.

"It seems," said Bogna thoughtfully one evening, "that the human pack-horse can stand rather a lot. Just where *is* the proverbial end of one's tether?"

Those random heavy jobs were wearing us out, and when, on 6 March 1942, Hermina put us to work in the Sanitation block, we were quite relieved. But by now we had a motto: things are never so bad that they can't get even worse.

At first, however, we were hopeful, and at least the spring rains were easier to bear indoors. But even this stupefyingly boring work of assembling, measuring and stitching bituminous paper sheets for the wounded was beyond our strength. Still, at least it made some kind of sense. It was, after all, for the benefit of human beings. But 'red' Krystyna disagreed: "What do you mean, human beings?" she protested. "They're Germans."

I thought about that for quite a long time – all through the night-shift – and then replied: "You know, in the end it comes to the same thing. A wounded soldier on a winter's night will freeze no matter which side he's on, and our covers may at least help to warm him."

"Warm the Germans! Are you crazy?" A heated discussion broke out in which the word 'hatred' was freely used. She hated them, Alicja said furiously; and she flew at me in a rage when I said that I felt no hatred at all. Was it true? Yes, it was, but I shall never be able to understand why. There in the camp I felt no hatred for the Germans, and I feel none now. Whenever I met a German, I would look at him with unusual interest; stare at him, really. Perhaps I was trying to find some traces of humanity in him. And sometimes I did catch a glimmer. Even when a German woman was bashing me about the head, I was still curious about what made her behave like that. What were her feelings at that moment? And what were ours? Was it really only hatred?

One day, the most brutal of all our overseers was walking along the camp street with her child who was wearing a red coat. (It was the first time I'd seen a young child in the camp.) A little, bright-haired blonde child with a big, bright-haired, blonde woman. The woman was looking at her child with a tenderness we would never have suspected her capable of; and when she spoke, it was in a tone of such gentleness that for a moment we wondered if we had mistaken her for someone else. A soft, warm voice. You should have heard her when she was yelling at *us*!

We were no longer 'new girls' as the camp had gradually yielded up its secrets to us. We knew which Germans were the worst, which work-teams the most demanding; and we had got to know some of the camp VIPs. But we were still, for all that, a grey, haggard, rag-bag collection of women who were growing hungrier by the day. We were painfully thin, and had begun to talk endlessly about food. Hunger obsessed us even more than the craving for sleep. (If you're hungry, you can't sleep anyway.) We couldn't really have said which of the two pains was worse.

But it is the hunger I remember most, or rather the effects of it. Those were dreadful days. Gaunt-faced women, their eyes glistening as though from fever, hallucinating about food. It would start quite innocuously with reminiscing about a concert or a play. And then came the inevitable question: And where did you have supper afterwards? And off they went. They would expound at length and in immense detail on the best way of stuffing a turkey. They drank in every word with a kind of morbid greed. Some of them wrote every word down, and afterwards would invite us all to an imaginary feast where they would read the items aloud. Elegant hors d'oeuvres to start the menu, then wine, a meat dish, and, to finish, a dessert of ice cream.

Instinctively we drew back from these conversations, and did our best to avoid them. We were sorry for those women, but they aroused our fear and disgust too, because we were terrified of becoming like them. Strangely enough, *I* didn't feel particularly hungry, or, at least I never experienced hunger as a raging torment. But I got thinner and weaker all the time. (I never saw myself in a mirror, but I could see what Krysia looked like.) It filled us with terror to see women who, in prison and during our quarantine, had talked about literature, art and life, now talking only about food and in no state to think about anything else. Some dreamed of good, solid food with which to stuff themselves, others drooled at the thought of gourmet dishes; some wanted puddings, others only snacks. They wrote down recipes in different languages or recited recipes into their pillows before going to sleep.

I loathed that talk and that gluttony-obsessed atmosphere. Were human beings really no more than the sum of the calories they consumed?

But how can the well-fed understand about hunger? You need to experience in your own person what it means to be so hungry that you can't sleep; to be faint with hunger and watch your muscles wasting away as we were doing, day by day. We could estimate our strength from the cooking-pots. In the early days, we didn't have to stop once as we carried them from the kitchen to the block. But now we had to keep stopping more and more often to get our breath back; we could hardly take them any distance at all. Carrying a cooking-pot – such a trifling and insignificant object – yet how much pain those things caused us, how much exhaustion and humiliation, how many cuffs and slaps. "Pick it up; get going; quickly; at the double." Those hated phrases. For four whole years we existed in one headlong rush, driven on by blows: I hurry because I have to, because if I don't I'll be hit over the head or sent to the punishment block or to a penal work unit . . .

We young ones had to carry the cooking-pots because the older women lacked the strength. We had always done so. But when our muscles wasted and we were scarcely able to carry the things at all, we rebelled, or rather our exhausted bodies did. Some of the others supported us, saying that the young ones ought to be excused on the grounds that they were still growing and had their lives in front of them; or because they had never been used to hard work and couldn't cope with it as their elders could. But many of the older prisoners did not agree, and there were frequent rows about the subject.

We didn't want to give in, so we gritted our teeth, and again I thought of that inner resolve which had come to define our humanity. I must, simply *must* get the better of my hungry body. I *will* not stop being myself just because I am hungry. We women 'politicals' had our pride. But hunger is a terrible thing, monstrous and indescribable. When I think of all the vile tricks and petty betrayals to which it drove so many of us . . . 'Thou shalt not steal when thou art hungry.' Yes, but why not? Why go on fighting this endless battle for mastery over oneself?

And do you know the greatest temptation of all? To give up the struggle, to give up thinking once and for all.

7

One day towards the end of March, when we got back from work, we found that our block had simply ceased to exist. It had been divided up among other blocks. And only then did we appreciate how that ghastly alien crowd of bickering women had become our friends; familiar, close and dear to us. But now? No longer were we in our spotless Polish block, and we understood too late the mutual tolerance with which 'our girls' had conducted their quarrels, the extraordinary refinement of their conversation. Compared, that is, to what awaited us in block 16.

A barracks full of prostitutes and thieves of every nationality; coarse, screaming harridans. We were afraid of them. Not to put too fine a point on it, we were scared rigid. No possibility here of poetry readings, or cultural evenings – nor even of harmless culinary droolings.

Mercifully, they moved us out again at Easter. The Germans often marked the feasts of the Church in this way, arranging some special transport or a block search.

The new block wasn't Hell; only Purgatory. Hell was to come next, two weeks later, when they transferred us yet again. This time they sent us to block 11.

Block 11. I go cold at the mere thought of it . . . those women . . . the block where we first understood the full hideousness of that odd word 'elel' – LL – the initials of lesbian love.

Within a few days that band of women had completely terrorised us. They stole everything we had: only half our camp rations ever reached us and soon those last souvenirs of freedom – our toothbrushes and combs, together with the few treasures we had brought with us from prison – vanished irretrievably. We couldn't wash, because they wouldn't let us into the wash-room. We couldn't go to the sleeping-quarters during the day, because the woman in charge wouldn't let us. She was always 're-making' our beds, stealing anything she could find and spitting on the sheets. It was horrible to have to lie on those sheets after she'd spat all over them.

I managed to shield Krysia from seeing some of what took place while that word, 'elel', acquired a hideous, inhuman reality. Whatever will become of us? I asked myself. A couple of years from now, will we be like that too?

I don't really know if Krysia understood why I stopped giving her a goodnight kiss. Maybe she even resented my not doing so. But the incredible goings-on in that block destroyed my faith in the innocence of even the simplest human gesture. I gave up believing in affection or purity.

Often at night it took me ages to get to sleep. At first I couldn't credit what was happening, and watched wide-eyed, torn between curiosity and despair.

The last shreds of humanity were slowly disappearing. Lesbian love . . . love . . . love . . .

A few days later, a note was pressed into my hand by a gypsy. "If you want to," Zorita had written, "come to the corner of block 12."

Zorita had seemed like a gentle girl, with great, black, velvety eyes. Only now did I understand the meaning of those inviting glances. My first reaction was to laugh: so I was to play the man, was I? But the laughter died still-born. It was horrible, and sad. And I wanted no part in it.

I stopped looking in Zorita's direction. She was tiny and thin – but then we were all thin. But sometimes I would accidentally catch her eye, and what I saw there made me frightened. I recoiled at first, but soon began to feel pity.

Propositions came thick and fast. Apparently I was in demand as a woman as well as a 'man'. I felt hemmed in, constantly threatened. Women who at first had recoiled in disgust, little by little gave up the unequal struggle. It spread like a plague . . . like a bush-fire . . . like a consuming passion. I looked on, terrified, and concentrated my efforts on preventing Krysia from seeing the worst of what was happening.

But in the end, of course, she did see. How could she *not* see those awful scenes when they were actually being enacted by our own bedside. She cried for a long time that night and never again came to say goodnight to me in bed; at least not in the same way as before.

Sometimes we had to work at night, and then we would see less of it. On the other hand, our block-leader and her charming side-kick wouldn't let us sleep. I can't bring myself to repeat the curses that they rained on us, day in, day out. Anyway, it doesn't matter now. Whichever way you look at it, life in that block crushed us totally, extinguished us. Even the Germans had stopped sending the worst offenders to the punishment block which was full to over-flowing. We had less and less of the will to live, more and more of loathing, exhaustion and the desire to escape – no matter where. After that we sank into an utter indifference in which abuse simply ran off us. What did any of it matter? With a last faint glimmer of the urge for self-preservation, we withdrew from our surroundings into an interior world of our own. We talked to no one, avoided all contacts. Nothing else mattered except getting through that day, and then the next. Yesterday had already gone. To lie down, to sleep, to forget, even for a brief moment, was all we cared about.

It was from that hellish block that the first thirteen of us went to their deaths. 18 April 1942. Until then, they hadn't taken anyone out of our transport and we had convinced ourselves – quite unjustifiably – that death sentences were carried out only at the Castle. We were sure that, in being sent to the camp, we had at least been saved from the danger of execution.

It was a beautiful sunny day when they took the thirteen, all of them friends of ours. We knew their backgrounds, so we were anxious when we heard their names read out; but we refused to believe the worst. They turned and looked at us as they walked away, towards the big square in front of the administrative offices. Mila waved, and Pola pointed towards the sky.

Tall, slender Pola, and Grażyna too, the two Chrostowski sisters. Grażyna who not long ago had written the poem about the sunflower which used to peep in at us that first foul September of our quarantine.

Niusia Apcio – arrested by mistake for someone else, because her real name was Maria and she worked in a chemist's shop.

Genia Adamiak, a shy civil servant who worked in a town hall somewhere, pale and always pleasant, though fussy and forever worried about something or someone.

Maria Waśniewska with her black, restless eyes, thin, trembling hands and slightly husky voice which always sounded nervous and strained. Yet now suddenly she was utterly calm.

Renata Żytkowa, slim, tall and fair, forever talking about her little son whom she'd had to leave behind with strangers . . .

Kazimiera Banowa and Zofia Grabska, less well-known to me, but at that moment every bit as dear . . .

Romka, our delightful Romka, bubbling with life and fun, lively as quicksilver, loved wherever she went . . .

Mila, little Mila Radecka with her huge eyes and bird-like nose.

Mrs Wersocka who went calmly, even joyously. All her family had been executed, and she alone had remained.

They went . . .

The Germans locked them in the Bunker first of all, and then, stripped of their headscarves and overalls, barefoot and wearing nothing but thin dresses, they were loaded into the 'mini' – our name for the small black car which from then on came so frequently to take away the condemned.

Ravensbrück had not yet acquired its own gas chamber.

Executions took place on Death Row behind the camp wall. The victims faced a firing squad there, and the noise of the rifle shots rang out over the whole camp.

They went . . . and their blood-stained dresses were sent to the laundry – irrefutable proof that they would not be coming back: poor Pola who had been so sure that one day she would be going home; and Niusia who used to weep for fear that she would not. Their turn today – whose turn would it be tomorrow?

The thought of that tomorrow cast a fearful new shadow over us. Until that day we had not really considered the possibility of execution. But now we saw clearly: our friends had died today, and tomorrow might be our turn. On 18 April death came close, and thereafter never left our side. Many times we believed that the end had come, and each time we reacted differently: sometimes in panic; sometimes with downright longing – anything to get out of this hell-hole; sometimes we faced the prospect with a shrug and a 'so what?' But at other times we rebelled, wanting to do something, anything, to escape, not just wait for certain death like meek lambs for the slaughter; to take matters into our own hands for once instead of passively accepting our fate. I wanted to live, to become a human being again rather than prisoner number 7709.

In those days, when we lived in the shadow of death, we came to view everything with a completely new perspective. Nothing had any importance. We looked back on our lives and felt sad that we had achieved so little, sad that we were going to die, with nothing to leave behind but silly, senseless lives.

My friends of that time are dead, though I treasure them in my memory. But I still wonder why I, and not they, am still alive. When I came back from the camp, Niusia Apcio's mother asked me to go and see her. But I couldn't face her. What could I have said? Could she have seen me standing there and not felt bitter? Why was it I who had come back and not Niusia? No, no, no. I must stop myself thinking along those lines, and get back to my story.

After that first execution, an unusual quiet prevailed.

The others probably felt as I did, and like me they were determined not to be morbid. They took refuge in black humour. "Jim will be on fire with passion right now," laughed 'Rudampa', pointing at the crematorium chimney. But few of us slept that night. I couldn't stop thinking of Mila who was so tiny that she couldn't reach the shelf for her soup-bowl. Showing Władka her palm one day, she had said: 'Look at that short life line. It must mean that I'm going to die young." No, I can't yet write about little Mila – the pain is too raw, even now.

8

The camp continued to hold us firmly in its nightmarish grip. Apart from anything else, our working conditions deteriorated. Our Sanitation block was transferred to the former block 15 and we were given a terrible overseer, a brutal German peasant woman.

I remember a broiling hot day when we had to carry enormous rolls of bitumen paper weighing over three hundred kilos each. I found it exceptionally difficult and felt awful. I think I was just ill. The wheels of the cart on which we were dragging these rolls sank deep into the powdery sand; six of us pushed it with all our strength, but could not shift it. The wheels sank right to the axle. I was angry, ill, exhausted and sweating, and the task was quite beyond my powers. But for all that, we kept on pushing. Suddenly our overseer was towering above us. Without warning, she struck me in the face. Though I had often been beaten, I had never been struck on the face before by a woman, or at least not in a way that seemed like a deliberate slap. This blow was carefully aimed. In vain did I tell myself that it was nothing, just one more blow among so many others. But it was worse than that; the pain was of an entirely different order.

Everyone in the camp knew that the Polish women were especially sensitive about slaps, and the guards often inflicted them as a special humiliation for women who were already too weak to respond. That slap, inflicted on a scorching day when I was feeling exhausted and ill, was the last straw for me. I had had enough and wanted to hit back. I remember gritting my teeth . . . but instead of lashing out at that woman, I went on meekly trying to push the cart. A beast of burden, a number, unrecognised and without honour. I had the appalling, terrifying conviction that I no longer existed, that they had killed me, that there remained not a single trace of the person I had once been. I was nothing but a broken shell.

The other girls did not look in my direction; they dared not so much as glance at me. I knew what they were thinking. I myself had often seen a friend being beaten, so I knew that they had all felt that desire to hit back, and had all found that they could not do it.

We did eventually reach the stage where none of the camp police dared to hit us in the face, and when even the overseers desisted. But that was later. In our present state, we were fair game for any humiliation.

Another restless night. It was such a trivial thing – a single slap; and yet it kept me awake till morning, in spite of my total exhaustion.

Still, I must admit that the slap may not have been the only reason for my sleeplessness. That day when we pushed the giant rolls of paper in the broiling heat, I really was ill. For some time a huge inflamed abscess had been developing under my arm, and on that day the pain became so intense that I could not move it. Perhaps that is an exaggeration. I have written 'could not', and yet I had moved that arm all day long as I worked. I had no choice. As a result I passed a terrible night, and when I eventually slept, my dreams were woven of strange fantasies, a mingling of past memories and future longings. I remember that I dreamed of a blue sailing boat with orange sails. And of the waters of a lake. I awoke to find the swelling so enormous that I could scarcely move my arm. And together with this burning fever this forced them to send me to the rewir – the camp hospital.

The rewir was crowded with suffering people, and all queueing for attention. It was the first time I had seen Dr Oberheuser at close quarters. She seemed pleasant enough, a fair-haired woman, quite pretty but unremarkable. When I stared at her, she didn't scream at me to stop; her voice was quiet and extremely courteous. She looked at my arm without a word, but without gentleness either. In fact, her touch was quite unnecessarily firm. Then quite without warning – she lanced the swelling. The pain was agonising, but I neither gasped nor flinched; just stood there gritting my teeth. Only then did she look at me carefully, and asked – or rather stated: "A Polish girl, naturally." The nurse, herself Polish, answered for me, in German: "Yes, she is." Summoning my last remaining strength, I went out of the rewir. Big drops of sweat glistened on my brow. I sat down on a step for a moment, and was immediately moved on by a camp policewoman. I dragged myself off to work. My head was spinning, and I was still feverish but no one took my temperature. Next day, when I returned to the rewir for a second dressing, my temperature was sky-high, 39.7 degrees Centigrade (102°F). But it made no difference; I still had to go back and work all day. My overseer didn't deign to notice either my fever or my pain. Only Krysia looked devastated and kept stealing anxious glances in my direction.

I don't remember how long that abscess lasted, but I do remember all the nights I couldn't sleep for pain. I suddenly found myself remembering a day when my mother hadn't wanted me to go to school because the thermometer was registering 37.4 degrees centigrade (99°F). Was it possible that such a time had ever existed?

Of course I wasn't the only one who had to work with a raging temperature. There were many other women in the same boat as myself, and mine was not the only abscess that Oberheuser had lanced that day. Abscesses were quite common among the starving and exhausted prisoners.

Nobody gave a damn, however. They sent the contagious sufferers to the rewir, and the ones who had simply collapsed. But if you were still capable of standing up, you didn't need treatment, let alone permission to stay in bed.

The so-called 'bed-cards' were hard to come by. I was only ever given one once, and that was much later. Right now, I had to stand in a queue with countless other nameless women, for primitive medical treatment brutally administered. This didn't really matter – obviously it was going to hurt – but I have never forgotten how roughly they removed those dressings. Only then did I begin to understand those warnings about the rewir which had been given to us while still in quarantine: but how much I still had to learn, to endure.

9

The days succeeded each other with deadly monotony. Today I wonder how those seemingly identical days could in reality have been so different from each other; for paradoxically, it was precisely on those days when nothing appeared to happen that so much actually did.

Time was measured in strange ways, which bore no resemblance to the ways we had once known. Saturdays were tremendously important, for that was when the letters were distributed.

When a white postcard came from home, it was hard to believe that that little scrap of paper had actually come from there. It was already a different world. Our families and friends wrote as though everything was going on as usual. Someone had got married, someone had died, someone else had given birth. Life was carrying on without us. But their affectionate words, telling us that they loved us, were waiting for us, missed us sorely, warmed our frozen hearts with emotion.

And all we could send by way of reply was the regular monthly message, in German: "I am in good health and spirits." Those lying words were graven on our souls.

Spring came in all its beauty. Glorious, splendid, rich in colours and scents. Even in the camp the perfume of certain flowers reached us, and we could see the geese flying low over the lake. I resolved that, if ever I returned home, I would spend every free moment just wandering about. Every holiday and every Sunday, drinking in my precious freedom.

One day, as a punishment, I was sent to a penal work-unit to unload bricks from a boat. I had a full view of the lake sparkling in the sunlight. It was so beautiful. And we stood there in a chain, throwing bricks to each other. It was the first time I had ever done this particular task, and I didn't know how to avoid cutting my hands on the bricks' sharp edges.

After a couple of hours, my hands were skinned raw, a mass of bleeding flesh and on every brick I touched I left an outline of my bleeding fingers. As the pain became intolerable, I bit my lips until the blood flowed. When I could stand it no more, I let my hands drop, and watched the blood stream down on to the ground and be swallowed up by the golden sand. The pile of bricks in front of me mounted by the minute. "What's going on?" shrieked the overseer. I said nothing but lifted my hands for her to see. She pulled me out of the line and silently stood me to one side. For the rest of the day I was put to carrying baskets. Even that was horribly painful.

I remember the horrified faces of Władka and Krysia when I got back to the block . . . My hands went on hurting. They were given no chance to heal because every day they were forced to do hard labour. One particularly deep wound turned septic and went on festering for a long time. It left behind an odd-looking scar which I still have.

Officially it was now summer, so they took away our warm clothes and shoes, leaving us barefoot and with nothing but thin summer dresses to wear. We froze all through the morning and evening roll-calls. The sun scorched us during the day, but after sunset it was very cold. Even in winter we had not endured such cold as during those first weeks of the Ravensbrück 'summer'.

In the icy air and early morning light, I looked around at the familiar faces. Dear God, what had happened to them? The girls' faces were long and pallid, with no trace of colour; their bodies were thin, their eyes without hope. Those eyes . . . the huge eyes of a crowd of emaciated women had to be seen to be believed. We were all eyes – nothing else of us remained.

I spotted just one rosy face with rounded cheeks – one of the cooks – and felt the stirrings of envy. That one wasn't hungry, I thought – unlike the rest of us.

In June, fresh transports arrived, and once again there

were strange women milling about the place. A 'new camp' was set up, block 21. Grey-haired women who had just arrived from Poznań looked us over disparagingly. Just as we had once done ourselves.

They had long ago taken our bedding away. We were now sleeping two to a bed on Saturdays, and on other days taking it in turns to lie on the dirty, grey straw pallets. There was less and less to eat, and never any salt. It was horrible, but we ate whatever they gave us, even the revolting sour cabbage which for a long time we couldn't bring ourselves to swallow.

Dinner – the daily soup of turnips or potato peelings or kale, or, very occasionally, porridge. In the mornings we drank our watery soup quickly – we never had enough time – and were hungry again almost immediately. Up to this time we were still peeling potatoes and throwing away the peelings; but the time was at hand when our starving companions would devour these scraps avidly.

It was awful to have no salt, and at first we simply couldn't eat even the little we were given without it. Then, of course, hunger quickly asserted itself, and we began to eat everything we could lay hands on. But the quantity of food grew steadily less. A loaf that had once been cut into four was now cut into six, then into eight, then twelve, and finally into eighteen, which meant one thin slice apiece. But that was towards the end.

Dividing up the bread was always quite a ritual. It had been like that even in the prison. There the Germans had distributed bread that was already cut into chunks but not divided up; so one chunk would have to be shared among a number of women – a very responsible task.

But that prison bread had been wonderful – real Polish bread; dark and made from rye. Ravensbrück bread was dreadful; it had the consistency of sawdust and smelled of fish-bones (they probably *did* add fish-meal to the dough). Still, it *was* bread, and in any case we had almost forgotten what that Polish bread tasted like.

Once again the ritual of sharing out bread. The women had eyes everywhere; never have I seen such terrible, darting eyes. There were innumerable quarrels and fights over those pathetic crusts, over whether one piece was accidentally bigger than another. If a woman made a mess of the job, she was never again asked to do the share-out, and felt properly humiliated.

In our group, it was little Krysia's job, and she was punctilious to a degree. She was so meticulous that no one ever found fault with the way she shared out the bread. Sometimes she and I ended up with a rather ragged slice, a bit the worse for wear. And as the hunger got worse, Krysia put even more effort into her careful bread-cutting. At times her hand shook and beads of sweat gathered on her upper lip and brow. But it couldn't be helped; it was part of the price we paid for being trusted.

Bread soon became the only worthwhile currency. For a long time there was no barter in our camp (I say 'our' because later, when large numbers of Auschwitz prisoners came to swell our numbers, we became rather provincially patriotic about belonging to Ravensbrück) – but as time went on the practice grew. Smokers would sometimes sacrifice their day's ration of bread for cigarettes, which somehow or other were always available, while we used to swap our bread for medicines and sometimes even for books.

I remember how we paid through the nose for that first book. We bought it blind, because we had no alternative, from a Ukrainian woman who had access to the stolen property wagons. Our go-between, who was quite illiterate, was to choose a book for us at the huge cost of four bread rations. And it was beautiful. Leather-tooled with gilt edging: a Greek–Russian dictionary. Our Ukrainian had thought it was the prettiest of all the books she had found, and couldn't understand why our faces registered disappointment. Anyway, we found a few enthusiasts for the book and gave it to them for nothing. And, thankfully, our Ukrainian improved in time.

10

Throughout June 1942, and even more in July, before the
summer had really got going, we almost froze to death.
The morning roll-calls were very cold, and the ground
after the freezing nights struck chill into our feet. One
bright girl hit on the idea of cutting out feet from paper
and wearing them. It worked for a few days – that thin
layer of paper was unimaginably warm. But the overseers
quickly pounced on our 'invention' and beat us severely
for this latest example of 'sabotage'.

By July 1942 we were like lethargic skeletons – with no
colour in our cheeks, our necks long and scrawny, our
features sharp. But not even the sight of all the naked,
skinny 'old' women in the wash-room could rouse me to
disgust any longer. We had learned to look without
emotion not only at our own and other people's emaciated
bodies, but even at those who collapsed and died. We could
react to nothing at all.

In an attempt to assuage our hunger, we would make a
superhuman effort to stock-pile our bread during the week
so as to have a feast on Saturday and Sunday. All week we
would carry around scraps of bread in a little bag made out
of sewn-together handkerchiefs, looking longingly at them
and licking our lips furtively in anticipation.

On Saturday and Sunday we would have a 'blow-out',
doing our miserable best to recreate home conditions. A
rinsed-out duster did duty as a tablecloth, and the teaspoon-
ful of jam, lump of hard cheese and cube of margarine that
had been given us for supper were turned into tastefully-
prepared sandwiches which expressed the personalities of
those who had made them. Nina liked to spread all her jam
on one thick wedge, while Bogna cut hers into microscopi-
cally thin slices so as to have as many as possible. But even

Bogna was outdone in sophistication by the apparently guileless Krysia who kept all her margarine and jam to spread on the very last slice, 'to make it taste like cake'. I was her partner in crime, since Krysia made up those mouth-watering slices for both of us. Everyone agreed that Krysia was a marvellous person – always so kind and gentle and well-behaved that no one could possibly find fault with her. But, according to Hermina we were all mistaken. Only Hermina had seen Krysia as she really was; "Krysia is a big mouth," she said. (On one occasion during Hermina's reign there had been an unholy row when, in the darkness, she blamed Krysia for a cheeky retort. And from then on we used to tease Krysia about it – even though I was the one responsible – and the legend of her 'big mouth' spread all through the camp.)

At moments like that we could console ourselves that some remnant of our essential selves still lurked beneath the striped uniforms. If it had not been so, would Stenka always have been able to out-run us, always arriving first no matter where we went? No, that was a secret power belonging to Stenka alone. After roll-call she was always first back to the block, and even though we raced, we would get to the wash-room to find Stenka already half-naked and covered in soap, standing there smiling at us. We always had to wait for her to finish. We suspected her of being in contact with 'unclean spirits', especially as she never seemed to exert herself. Some keen-eyed observers were almost prepared to swear that she arrived before her own shoes. It *was* incredible, though we did rather exaggerate the bit about the unclean spirits, since Stenka was always fastidiously clean. Though, perhaps even she was not as clean as Bogna who was renowned throughout the *whole* camp for her cleanliness. Bogna used to fret because there was no flame over which she could burn out the impurities that infested our horrible, unhealthy bread.

There was another thing, too, that helped convince us we were still human: verses of poetry for which we dredged our memory. Joanna's head was a positive gold-mine; a nugget would suddenly pop out, a solitary stray verse which she would toss around in her head until the next bit emerged, but not necessarily in the correct order. She would juggle them about, till at last she cried: "Right, girls, I've got it!" Then for a moment we were able to tear ourselves away from our nightmare lives while Aloha laughed up at us from a palm-fringed beach, Cassiopeia leaned out of the starry sky towards us, or the crippled little shoemaker beckoned to us. And afterwards the 'much-loved clear and simple song of the cherubim' would ring out, and our grey day would finally end on a note of hope. Then in the silence we would whisper a prayer: 'Rescue our country from this terrible war; grant peace to those who are in anguish.'

Dreams were a personal, secret domain where few could penetrate. In time we – the 'grey throng of the uninitiated' – came to know that to dream of plums meant bruises; fire meant a thief; eggs represented idle gossip, while mushrooms denoted freedom, as did indigestion and scrubbing floors.

Our dreams fell into two categories. The more usual kind were what Manicha scornfully dismissed as 'sexual' and our 'experts' described as Freudian. The second kind were strange, intuitive dreams that would come suddenly to one person, then spread to us all, carrying with them an unmistakable aura of death. Always, just before an execution, this weird, formless sensation would inexplicably grip us and without a word being spoken, we all knew that something was about to happen. None of us ever gave voice to these premonitions of death, but at roll-call the silence would be deeper and more intense than usual, the prayers more fervent. The shadows under our eyes became even more pronounced and our voices would unaccountably break. Then the names would be read out. A few, not many. We were no longer under any illusions about the meaning of Special Transport, and we understood only too well why we were never allowed outside the camp perimeter. Our whole transport had to stay within the camp confines under strict supervision, so that the latest victims could be extracted from the ranks without fuss. Our whole transport now lay under sentence of death.

11

Throughout July 1942 our dreams and forebodings ran riot. On 27 July our transport was ordered to the main square. First the under-twenty-fives, then the rest. Later on, they added some of the May 1942 transport to our number. A group of visiting officials, civil and military, came and made a close examination of our legs. After we'd stood there for a few hours, they finished checking their list and sent us back to the block in time for the midday meal.

All through that afternoon, our imaginations worked overtime. A woman's capacity for fantasy is boundless; I doubt if anyone has ever discovered its limits. And by the end of that day, we had plenty of theories to choose from, all from 'an impeccable source'. One theory, put about by the incurable optimists, confidently asserted that an exchange of prisoners was about to take place and that we would be in the first transport to Switzerland. A second – this one from the hard-core pessimists – predicted a mass execution.

Early the next day we were summoned to the rewir. When we caught up with our own group, the others were already standing in line. I joined the last row of five. They took the first ten, and then found they were one short. Ignoring the next row of five, they came to my row and led me away from the end. All I could think was that this time I was on my own. Krysia was not there.

Inside the rewir, nothing much happened. We were ordered to take off our clothes. Dr Oberheuser and Dr Rosenthal weighed us, looked at our hands and legs as though examining us for infectious sores, and that was all. As I left, the camp siren wailed out the midday break. The examinations were over for the day, and we were sent back to the block.

Two days later, one of the camp messengers came in with a list of names. She had come to fetch the ten women who had already been examined. Anna, our block-leader, shrugged and said she knew nothing about it. All she told us was that we were to present ourselves at the rewir.

There were three from our block. I could see Krysia's pale face at the window as we left, and Sledzia's, briefly flushed, next to hers.

I had just come off night work. In spite of that, or perhaps because of it, the colours all around me seemed particularly vivid. The scarlet salvias in front of the rewir seemed to scream at me.

Inside, we immediately bumped into Dr Rosenthal. Who are these people? he asked. "The ones you sent for," said Anna. The other seven were already there. The doctor counted them – and sent four back to their block.

That left six of us. We stood there for some time, and I looked to see who my companions were. We'd all been charged with resistance activities. So, then, it was now our turn at last. Execution. I remembered how they liked to stage little comedies, like taking the victims to the camp hospital for examination before shooting them, sometimes even pretending that they were being sent out on a transport, and handing out bread for the journey.

In a sense, I was relieved at the prospect of instant death, and even began wondering what it would feel like. I felt nothing else; no sense of something solemn or dramatic or momentous. This surprised me. Why was I so calm? Couldn't I summon up some feeling, when death was staring me in the face? I despised myself, and looked at the greenish-white face of Marysia Gnaś with sympathy. She caught me looking at her. "What are they going to do to us?" she whispered.

I shrugged and with a total lack of emotion came out with one of the phrases we had used in the Lublin jail: "Exterminate us."

In the eyes of that big strong girl I saw such insane terror that I immediately regretted my words.

"No, it can't be true!" she almost shrieked.

But again I only shrugged.

Then they summoned us to go inside. At that time I didn't know the exact lay-out of the rewir, so I didn't know what to expect. I went in first. It was a bathroom. A real white bath with real hot water.

My first proper bath in eighteen months! Quickly, I undressed – and a pale German woman came in and removed my clothes. A moment later she returned, with a clean night-dress and a dressing-gown. I asked her what it was all about, and she looked at me in terror:

"I suppose you must be ill, and they're going to operate."

"Nonsense. I'm as healthy as a horse."

She looked more terrified than ever.

I remember thinking only of her cowardice: that she was just too afraid – or ashamed – to tell me of my imminent execution.

Sister Frieda took me out of the bath and led me down a corridor to the end room, where six clean white beds were waiting. Noting with a certain ironic satisfaction that after all I *was* still capable of feeling, I acknowledged that I was frightened by the sight of those beds. Sister Frieda told me to lie down, but I stood there, undecided as to which bed to choose. I was sure they were going to finish us off with an injection rather than a bullet. Grimly, I lay down on the first bed on the right.

And in spite of everything, it felt extraordinarily pleasant to be lying in a clean bed. I was very tired, and longed for sleep.

One by one, the others came in and lay down on the left hand side: Wanda Kulczyk, Aniela Okoniewska, Rozalia Gutek, Marysia Gnaś and Maria Zielonka . . .

There was quite a lot of aimless chatter, but all I could think about was sleep. Then a scream brought me back to reality. I opened my eyes to see a dark-haired nurse bending over Wanda with a gleaming razor in her hand. I leaped out of bed. The nurse explained soothingly that she wasn't going to hurt Wanda, but was only intending to shave her legs. I translated this into Polish for the others and could hear the incredulity in my voice. Why on earth were they shaving our legs if they were going to put us to death?

One by one we were shaved from ankle to knee. And then Sister appeared with an injection – 5 cms of viscous yellow fluid. An intra-muscular injection. I knew that death could be induced by a mere 1 cm injected under the skin, so why so much?

After the injection, I felt heavy and inert. I could see and hear but not move. We lay there like stooks of mown hay. Were our muscles paralysed or something? None of it made any sense.

"What are they doing to us? What are they doing to us?" moaned Maryśia indistinctly, and the same question was mirrored in all our eyes.

Oh God, if only I could be certain they were going to kill us, that that was all they were going to do!

Sister came back yet again. Another injection, this time beneath the skin. First they had immobilised us; whatever were they doing now? An operating trolley was wheeled into the room, and I suddenly recalled the words of the little nurse in the bathroom. An operation, she had said. But what kind of operation? And why? What possible reason was there? I could make absolutely no sense of it at all.

They wheeled Wanda out on the trolley. We were left behind in the silent room, numb with apprehension.

Before long we heard them bring her back, but they left her lying on the trolley in the corridor outside. I gave up trying to understand, and fell asleep.

Much later that afternoon I woke with a fearsome headache. On the chair near the bed was a bowl of green kale. At the sight of it I felt quite ill.

Sister came in with a pile of clothes, ordering us to put them on at once and return to the block. What? To the block? I must have looked absolutely stunned, because she asked angrily: "What are you gaping at? I told you, get back to your block!"

I tried to walk, but could not: my legs buckled beneath me. Some Polish women who were working in the rewir helped us back to the block.

Our friends welcomed us with genuine joy. They had been sure we were already dead. The Mini had drawn up outside the rewir and they presumed we'd been loaded into it. Then too our dresses had been delivered to the laundry, as was usual after an execution.

I felt tearful at the sight of so many well-loved, familiar faces. They gathered round in a circle – those who knew us and those who didn't – and fired questions at us. I felt weak, but some of the women looked mistrustfully at me, asking:

"Are you sure that's all they did?"

"Are you sure you're alright?"

"Didn't they do anything to you while you were asleep?"

"Do you feel alright inside?"

"What about your head?"

What I felt inside was a suffocating anger, and eventually I retorted, speaking calmly with a sweet smile on my face:

"Well, of course, while I was asleep, they extracted my fifth screw, and I shall soon become rabid and start biting."

"There you are, didn't I tell you they would come back with a screw loose?" I heard someone behind me whisper triumphantly.

So they thought I was round the bend, did they? At that moment I wanted not only to bite, but to kick and scream. Fortunately for them, I also felt sick and dreadfully weak.

When the night-shift went off our block-leader announced that I was unfit for work. I lay in bed, feeling terrible, with red and green circles flashing in front of my eyes. Then the roll-call siren drove me to my feet.

I stood on the parade ground supported by Nina and Wojtka. "How dark it's getting," I thought, while Nina whispered in my ear, "Just hang on for one more minute." When the overseer had gone past, I collapsed in their arms. For the first time in my life, I fainted.

Next morning we were given 'bed-cards' for three days, and I lay in a chaos of whirling thoughts, caught up in a madly revolving succession of improbable fantasies. I was certain it wasn't over, certain that something frightful was in store. Speechlessly, I snuggled up close to Krysia. And then a wave of darkness swallowed me. I forced myself to calm down a bit, but my insides were churning with extreme fright. What did they intend to do next?

I felt as though I had died and come to life again; or alternatively, that I had lived through a hundred years in the space of less than three short days.

On Saturday morning, at 9 a.m. they came for us again. It was 1 August 1942.

12

The same six women, the same beds, the same dressing-gowns we'd left behind, the same injections – except that this time it was Wanda who returned unconscious on the trolley, with her leg in plaster up to the knee and a Roman 'I' painted on the plaster.

One at a time we were wheeled away on that trolley, weak and unresisting.

In the corridor outside the operating theatre, Dr Schidlausky anaesthetised us with an intravenous injection. Before I lost consciousness, a single thought chased round my mind: "But we're not guinea-pigs, for heaven's sake." I think I must have kept repeating this sentence throughout the operation, and afterwards Dziunia and some of the others took it up. No, a thousand times no, we were not guinea-pigs. We were human beings.

But the term stuck. We used it of ourselves, and soon the whole camp came to know us as 'the guinea-pigs'. The name was so apt that everyone, even the camp doctors, used it. To have spoken of 'the women whose legs were operated on' might have left room for doubt as to identity, but 'the guinea-pigs' left none at all.

When I came round, it was already late afternoon. The perimeter wall of the camp was casting a long shadow which reached the window of our room. I looked round at the others. Marysia Gnaś was sitting up, with a feverish flush on her round freckled face, while Wanda was gesticulating wildly. Only Zielonkowa lay immobile, for she was still unconscious.

I was desperately thirsty. The Sister passed me a white mug. I held out my hand to take it and was amazed that something so small could feel so appallingly heavy. I couldn't hold the mug and it fell with a crash and broke, scattering white fragments over the floor.

Consciousness began to flood back. I remembered my leg, and drew back the blanket. On the plaster were the letters III TK. I asked the others what was written on their cast: Wanda had I; Aniela I TK; Rózia II; Gnaś II TK; Zielonka III; and me III TK. The mystery deepened. I wasn't in any pain, but my leg was totally numb and my head ached with an unbearable heaviness.

Supper was brought in, the usual Saturday fare: stinking cheese and a piece of bread and margarine. Wanda ate a little of the food, so did Marysia Gnaś, but none of the rest of us could touch it. In any case, Wanda soon threw up.

I remember they brought me a letter from home; I looked at the white paper and felt puzzled at its strangeness. I couldn't read the words written on it, so I put it under my pillow. It was a few days before my eyes could focus properly again.

I longed for sleep. The hot, August night had already fallen. And that was when it all began! Suddenly the girls were no longer sitting up, they were lying in a semi-stupor, tossing and turning in all directions, trying to find a less painful position for their poor legs. But it was impossible: the slightest movement intensified that monstrous, intolerable pain.

Sleep abandoned us. Wanda was screaming, Rózia moaning quietly; and every so often Zielonkowa cried out: "O, Jesus . . ." Wanda's screams pierced my ear-drums and drilled into my brain until I thought I should go mad. "Shut up!" I shouted. She looked at me in an unfocused sort of way, and went on screaming. "Shut up!" I shouted again. "Shut up or I'll squash you to pulp."

A glimmer of understanding came into her fever-bright eyes: "I can't stop myself screaming," she said suddenly, quite calmly.

But she didn't go on screaming, just lay there groaning through clenched teeth. Anielka bit into her pillow and uttered the occasional long-drawn-out groan. Marysia

81

Gnaś cursed quietly and colourfully. Me? I wanted to swear, scream, cry out, everything. I was terrifyingly clear-headed. Sister looked in at us from time to time, and went away without a word. (Only our group, the first of the 'guinea-pigs', were fortunate enough to have a night-sister on duty. Our successors were simply locked in for the night, completely unattended.)

"She's waiting for us to die," I thought, seeing the SS woman's watchful eyes on us.

Outside the window I could see the black walls covered with hideously grinning barbed-wire. Here, not long ago, they had hung the charred body of a young gypsy girl who had tried to escape.

Wires, high tension wires. I spoke the words aloud, as my heart leapt with a sudden resolve. *If I can only touch those wires, I can be at peace. I shall not have to go on enduring this atrocious pain.*

I tried to stand up, but could not. I fell back on the bed with a resounding thwack, and Sister was there in a trice. "What's going on?" I didn't reply, for I was too busy concentrating on that urgent, driving thought: get to the wires, to the wires, to the wires . . .

Briefly I lost consciousness. In imagination the wires came closer, closer, till I could almost touch them. I could almost feel the blessed peace they would bring. "Is this death, then?" I wondered.

My body contorted violently. Someone was pulling at me, dragging at my pain-racked leg. I groaned aloud. The Sister rushed in, took one look at me, dashed out again and came back with a syringe. A little 1 cm subcutaneous injection. Followed by some drops. "They'll help the pain," she said, giving each of us the medication.

And it was true. The pain did ease a little, as though it had been wrapped round with cotton-wool, and one by one the girls fell asleep. Only Marysia Gnaś stayed awake. Through chattering teeth she kept on asking: "Can you see? There's someone there outside the window. He's coming for me." In spite of myself I looked over to the window, but could see only the faceless black night, the night without stars, as though for very shame it had averted its gaze.

That night a new longing was born. Longings came in a thousand shapes and colours and we were familiar with them all. They lived in our hearts and gnawed away at us, some of them like great red stinging ants, others more like huge vicious dogs, and others again that pricked our flesh with a thousand unseen needles. There were the scarlet kind, for love, for kisses and embraces; the golden, for happiness, home and warmth; the blue, for green woods, moors and meadows; and the green, for books, plays and music. There were also the lesser longings for black coffee, evening dresses, coloured fabrics: silly luxuries. And the tremendous silver longings for a mother's arms, for the sight of her grey hair, for the quiet of a church – or for one's own inner silence.

But this new longing was black, and it was for death. I longed to die, to cease to exist, to perish without trace, for an end to the eternal, obsessive self-questioning: why? what was it all for? And, worst of all, why me? why us?

Dawn had already broken when Marysia Gnaś fell asleep at last, and I too slowly drifted away into dreams. Coloured triangles chased each other before my eyes. "They're dancing," I thought. Dancing? The thought brought a renewal of pain. And what about me? What about us? Would we ever be able to dance again? What were they doing to our legs?

It was morning again. Sunday mornings were different from other days in that a radio loudspeaker was put up on the camp's main street. In a show camp like Ravensbrück, care was taken to provide 'cultural entertainment' for the prisoners. What a joke! The loudspeaker blared forth, blasting our ear-drums and dragging us out of sleep. The nauseating tones of Traümerei jangled our nerves. Sister came in to collect samples of blood and urine, samples which from now on she would take every second day. She put a thermometer into our mouths, and when she took out mine again I got a look at the silvery column of mercury and read out: "Just over 40 degrees Centigrade (104°F). Good heavens, I must be dreaming!"

Zielonkowa had a temperature of 40°C, and so did the others. Wanda's was the lowest at 39.7°C. So now I knew where Aniela's pretty rosy cheeks had come from.

That evening, as it began to grow dark, I spotted Władka's troubled face next to Krysia's at the window. They looked so pale. I couldn't get up, but I tried to smile at them.

Our legs swelled up, scarlet and angry. Mine was so swollen that the plaster cut into my flesh. A red streak ran up my right thigh all the way to the groin, where it ended in a painful lump. Dr Oberheuser came in with a notebook. She bent over each leg and sniffed, before making a careful entry in her book.

On Monday 3 August we had another visit from Dr Fischer, assistant to Professor Gebhardt who had performed the operations on us. He was a man in the prime of life, greying at the temples, with a surgeon's skilful hands. I surveyed him with interest, trying to discern some trace of feeling in his expressionless gaze. So that's what a man who has committed a cold-blooded crime looks like! Why? For what motive had he done it? Well, perhaps it was for the sake of advancing medical knowledge. Perhaps after all our pain was intended to serve a good cause.

Two other men followed Fischer: a young, elegantly-suited civilian, and an older military type. They asked us how old we were and why we had been arrested. Rózia said they'd arrested her because they couldn't find her brother; she was to all intents and purposes a hostage. Her fourteen-year-old sister had been arrested at the same time too, but she had later been released.

More and more men came to see us. There was always someone coming to look at our legs. As time went by, we learned to ignore them all.

On the day that Fischer first came to see us, they applied the first dressings. God knows what it actually was, but they called it a dressing. They removed the plaster and did something or other to the wounds. We weren't able to see, because they put sheets over our heads, but whatever it was, it certainly hurt. I felt as though there were two gaping holes in my leg: one on the ankle bone, the other higher up; and that they were extracting something from these holes, something which was responsible for this atrocious pain.

They bandaged our legs and replaced the plaster. And they did not remove either plaster or bandages till a week later – and then only in the case of the first two numbers. Zielonkowa and I had to wait for two weeks.

The days succeeded each other in unchanging monotony. Our temperatures stayed in the region of 39 to 40°C. Every time we tried to move our mutilated legs, an evil-smelling yellowish brown fluid would seep from under the plaster sheath. Zielonkowa always had a pool on her bed, with swarms of flies buzzing round it.

They no longer had to bend down to sniff our legs. Dr Oberheuser would wrinkle her nose whenever she came in: "It smells revolting in here." We stank with the sickly-sweet odour of pus and rotting flesh. Pus oozed out of a deep groove in Zielonkowa's leg. Quite apart from the wound itself, our muscles were wasting away from the effect of the discharge. We had pain in our legs and in our heads; and the morphine which they gave us, at first three times and then twice a day, had scarcely any effect on the terrible pain.

Sometimes one of our friends would come to the window. Krysia would stand there, pale and thin, trying to look cheerful. Władka would turn up bearing an apple or a handful of currants – I couldn't begin to imagine where or by what miracle she had come by them. We ate them immediately and the fragrant apple would momentarily drown the odour of pus. Władka sometimes brought us some freshly cut and salted milkweed, and ordered me to eat it because it contained phosphorus. Well, I forced the bitter herb down, not because I believed in its power to heal, but because I wanted to please Władka. She smiled with her hazel eyes, persuading me into eating the stuff, despite its bitter taste.

They did strange things to us in the rewir. I think that those who came after us also suffered as we did, though not in precisely the same way. It was not just a question of pain, but of the gnawing anxiety which tormented us in those first post-operative days. New unexpected problems suddenly faced us. We were undergoing a totally new experience and life had acquired a new and bitter taste. Uncertainty about the future, the fear of being crippled for life, and the monstrous unmerited pain thrust in front of us a host of new and unanswerable questions.

Outside, the girls clustered anxiously at the window. Władka later told me that she thought I was about to die, since I looked so awful. She did her best to save me from myself, sending me letters and cards on which she had written: stop worrying; stop thinking of anything at all. Remember the water-meadows alive with flowers, the glory of spiky yellow mullein and heather; and try to remember how the nightingales sang in the story when Rafał rode to exile.

But it was no use. Even sleep had become a thing of the past and the pain that now tormented me was more than just physical. I was searching desperately for the meaning of my present existence, for the meaning of what was now being done to me.

At the very top of one of our windows lived a spider. I watched it, seeing the tiny flies imprisoned in its glistening web. At night, when I momentarily dozed off, that spider would enter my dreams on huge, furry legs and with the face of Dr Fischer. And in those dreams I was always the helpless fly. The face would come nearer and nearer, as though it were on film, getting bigger and bigger, until it filled the whole screen and I could see nothing but that face. A spider with the face of a surgeon; and I, the pathetic fly, caught in its web by my right leg. Even today, this dream often returns to torture me.

Joanna sent me a tiny blue and white sailing-boat carved from the handle of a tooth-brush. And I got a letter.

It was a strange coincidence that my love-letter from Africa should have arrived just then. I had not heard from my boyfriend until that day, nor did I hear from him again – but this letter not only got through it even escaped the censor. I don't know by what devious route it came to me. My boyfriend wrote and told me about his new blue sailing-boat with orange sails . . . The coincidence was quite forceful – and that night I actually slept for the first time in ages.

I didn't die, and I didn't go mad. I even discovered a meaning for my own sacrifice and this resolved a great torment: I had been operated on, so that Krysia might be guaranteed a return home, so that she would not have to undergo an operation, so that her legs at least would not be destroyed.

It was later, when Krysia was in fact taken off to undergo an operation, that the most dramatic moment came. I thought then that I should die of anguish and terror. Yet somehow I never lost my certainty that one day she would return home safe and sound. And she did return, healthy and without scars. She was one of the very few Ravensbrück guinea-pigs who were not scarred for life.

13

At about ten o'clock in the morning someone from our block rushed to the window and whispered: "Transport to an unknown destination. Five women from Lublin." She wasn't able to say any more. Leo, one of the camp policewomen, had hit her in the face.

We lay there quite still as rapid footsteps approached us. A nurse-overseer came in. She looked at each of us in turn, then took out a card and read out a name: "Rozalia Gutek, get dressed!"

She went out again. Rózia's face was ashen and she burst into tears.

"It's not enough for them to carve me up, now they want to murder me."

She sobbed all the time she was getting dressed, and we were afraid to try and comfort her. When she finished dressing, Rózia sat on the bed, unable to stand.

The overseer returned:

"How long since the operation?"

"Ten days."

"Get undressed again and get back into bed."

We sighed with relief: Rózia had at least a temporary reprieve.

On 15 August, a stifling hot day, came another surprise. It was Our Lady's Feast Day, and during our time in the camp it always seemed that the worst rows and most dire experiences were somehow linked with feast days of Our Lady. Whether it was just another indication of German bad faith or mere coincidence, we didn't know. But we soon began to dread those Feast Days.

Ever since morning, we had felt that something was brewing. They had brought three bunk beds into our room, and transferred us on to them. That left three terrifyingly empty beds. Who would be occupying them? We already knew that there were to be more operations. It was a shattering realisation, since we had hoped that the whole nightmarish business would end with us.

One by one we were taken on the trolley to the theatre and laid on tables.

They removed the bandages and for the first time I could see the wounds they had inflicted on our legs. They were all in the same place, along the right tibia, 4–6 cms above the ankle – a cut about 115 cms long, its width increasing according to the number written on the plaster. I touched my own wound with my hand: it was very wide, yellowish-green and putrid. But Zielonkowa's was the worst.

We lay there for several hours. The tables were hard, and, in spite of the August heat, cold (we were clad only in thin nightdresses). Zielonkowa, who had been given a purgative in the morning, was writhing in agony. There were no bedpans and no one paid any attention to our shouts, though we could hear footsteps nearby and the sound of people talking.

When at last someone came, there were eleven of them. Eleven men. Eleven healthy men looking down at six defenceless women. They put our temperature charts and the results of our blood and urine tests on the sheets beside us.

It was the first time I had seen Professor Gebhardt at close quarters. He was fat, with a puffy face and little eyes like gimlets. He stood in the doorway, plump hands clasped behind his back, while Dr Fischer came to each of us in turn, pointing and explaining. When it was my turn, he said: "The little one understands German," and continued his monologue in a whisper which I could not catch. He came closer and I could see traces of blood and plaster on his white overall. "Ah," I thought, "he's come here straight from the operating theatre." All eleven of them leaned over me, sniffing excitedly at my putrid wound. I glared at them with what I hoped was defiance and boundless contempt.

89

Then they went, leaving the door open; and we were left lying there. At length, the sound of voices and footsteps died away, and Oberheuser came and ordered us to get up immediately and go back to our room. I stared at her in disbelief, and pointed out that our legs were unbandaged and that for the last five hours the flies had been feasting on them. "So what?" came the reply.

She summoned a nurse who proceeded to bind up our legs in a desultory fashion. (Until now, they had been carefully bandaged every other day.) Then Oberheuser repeated her earlier command: "Get up and be off with you. Quickly."

Wanda was the first to jump down. Her right leg was so shrivelled that she could barely touch the floor with her toes, let alone stand on it. She bit her lip and, supporting herself against the wall, began to hop towards the door on her left leg.

Anielka, Rózia and Marysia followed suit. Zielonkowa groaned and, unable to contain herself any longer, relieved herself in the middle of the room. Two German nurses grabbed her under the armpits and half-dragged, half-carried her away.

"Get a move on!" Oberheuser was standing over me: "Hop, if you can't walk."

I was standing by the table on my left leg, and I felt unbelievably weak. For two weeks I'd had nothing but water and the handful of currants that Władka had brought me. The sweat poured down my brow as I tried to hop. Oberheuser continued shouting at me to get a move on, but I shrugged and spoke quite calmly:

"As you see, madam, I simply cannot."

She obviously did see, for she looked round quickly and, as no one was there, picked me up and carried me.

Further up the corridor, just short of our door, Wanda and Rózia were sitting propped up against the wall, breathing heavily and drenched in sweat. Dr Rosenthal emerged from another door, roared with laughter at the sight of them, then pulled them both to their feet and rushed up the corridor with one under each arm, their bandaged legs dragging along the ground. Even Maryśia Gnaś, the strongest one among us, had fallen halfway.

When we got back to the room, the new 'guinea-pigs' were lying in the room next door. Jadzia Kamińska had already come round from the anaesthetic and she smiled at me: "I haven't got any pain, you know." I nodded silently, knowing only too well what was in store for her. *I* hadn't had any pain, either, when I'd first come round.

It was almost evening when the other new 'guinea-pigs' began to wake. They laughed and joked, and my heart bled at the thought of what they would go through that night.

One of them, Krystyna Iwańska, didn't seem able to wake up. A sister came, took a look at her and slapped her twice on the cheeks. Krystyna didn't even flinch. Sister called Rosenthal. The lights were on by now, and the shutters had been pulled down. Rosenthal came in, swaying drunkenly, shirt buttoned wrongly over his hairy chest, sleeves rolled up. He took the syringe from Sister's hands, aimed at Krystyna's thigh – and stuck the needle into the pillow beside her. He laughed crazily, pinched Rózia on the cheek and lurched out of the room, still laughing. The Sister came back and gave Krystyna the injection. Not long after this, the girl came to and asked:

"Where's Jania?"

"In the next bed," I said.

"Ah," she muttered fuzzily, and went back to sleep again.

Sister brought in a bucket of water which she placed on the floor and then went out, locking the door behind her. I could hardly believe my eyes. Could they really be going to leave them there all night without attention? I looked round the room but the rest of our group were asleep after their gruelling day.

Urszula, who had been put in the bed nearest to my (top) bunk, opened her eyes and murmured something indistinctly. Suddenly she cried out: "Water, Duśka, please get me some water." And then she began raving, repeating over and over again in her delirium: "Krysia and

91

Duśka are wonderful, and so is Wieniuś. So is everyone, everyone's wonderful, except Hitler who's vile."

Nina, still only half-conscious, began to cry out loud. In the next room, I could hear the familiar sound of vomiting. I looked down from my upper bunk, and wondered how on earth I could reach the ground. Tying a corner of my sheet to the bed-rail, I slid down it – and landed on my bad leg! For a few minutes I sat there, unable to get to my feet. There were shouts of "Bedpan, bedpan!" from the next room. I hauled myself to my feet and, using the beds and walls for support, hopped into the next room and handed Maryśia a bedpan in the nick of time.

It got worse and worse. There was not enough water in the bucket, all the bedpans were full, and Nina was begging piteously for a drink. I banged on the door with my fists, I yelled, I pounded on the wall and on the shutters. But to no avail. Nobody came.

Soaking a rag in what remained of the water, I did what I could to moisten the lips of those who cried loudest for a drink. I was hopping unaided now, taking the shortest route from one bed to another. Behind me, a thin trail of brownish-yellow pus seeped on to the floor.

And so we continued through the night.

Just after the morning siren went, Władka came to the window.

"What on earth are you doing?" she cried out, seeing me standing there.

"I'm learning to walk. Oberheuser has ordered us to walk."

"Well, remember what I told you. Don't try too hard."

She gave me salted, chopped milkweed to eat, sandwiched between two pieces of bread.

Eventually, to my intense relief, a German woman arrived, and put me back to bed. Before dropping off to sleep, I realised that my previous day's inability to walk back to the room by myself must have been partly hysterical. If I'd really wanted to, I could have managed. The fact is, I hadn't wanted to enough.

After that, I began to eat and sleep again, and felt distinctly better.

Slowly our group of 'guinea-pigs' learned to walk again, while the others lay in a fever, their legs red and swollen. It happened with them exactly as it had happened with us: their temperature rose, according to the number written on the plaster. Nina was undoubtedly the worst sufferer.

On 23 August we were sent back to the block. Not that we could walk properly. Our wounds were still raw and suppurating. On our way out of the rewir, we passed Janka Mitura. They had operated on her that day – but with a difference. The incision was larger than ours had been, and there was no plaster on her leg.

So we went back to our places in the block, to filthy straw and no sheets. We could stand only with difficulty, but we were not given 'bed-cards', only 'indoor-work cards' and exemption from roll-calls. On her own initiative, our block-leader allowed us to stay in bed throughout the day. In doing so, she risked being reported, but, in spite of the danger, as long as we remained in her block, we were able to stay in bed.

We were cocooned in an atmosphere of good will. All the women tried to be as kind as they knew how. One of the outside workers brought us flowers, and another brought us some raw carrots. One day Fredzia Prusówna, a young girl from Zamość, smiled at me affectionately with her beautiful big eyes and threw her ration of bread on to my bed. "A treat, specially for you," she said, a radiant smile lighting her face. It was the last time any of us saw her. She went off to roll-call, and never returned.

On 1 September 1942 they took Aniela Sobolewska and operated on her. She was on her own, and she had both legs in plaster to the hip. The operation took a long time, over an hour. Listening behind the door of the operating theatre, Polish workers in the rewir heard the sound of bone being chipped away. Aniela did not have a high temperature, but she was in terrible agony. And not only from her legs; her whole body was racked with pain from lying immobilised on her back for so long.

Four days later, on 5 September, while the others were at early-morning roll-call, Aniela Okoniewska came to see me as usual. Her wound had healed, whereas I was still bed-ridden; so she used to come and keep me company in the empty block. A close friendship had sprung up between us. Blonde blue-eyed Aniela was as simple and fresh as a flower and used to talk to me about her little four-year-old daughter, of how she wanted to bring her up properly but was terrified that she would never see her again.

That day Aniela was unusually silent. Then suddenly, out of the blue, she asked:

"Do you think they will kill me? Me, who never did anyone any harm?"

I was shaken and said nothing. But Aniela went on:

"They can't harm me, because God will keep me safe. I have never in my life hurt anyone."

She stood by the window, her loveliness framed by the sky. She was praying.

That morning the latest list of those to be executed was delivered to the block. There were six names from our Lublin transport. Aniela's name was on it but had been crossed out with a red pencil. Aniela, very pale, just kept repeating: "I never did anyone any harm."

"And what about the other five?" I couldn't help thinking. "And Mila Radecka? Those who've already gone, and those who are about to go? Had *they* been guilty? Had *they* ever done anyone any harm?"

But I hid my thoughts and gave Aniela an affectionate hug.

That same day during the evening roll-call, we were once again sitting together. A volley of rifle shots followed by a series of short staccato bursts shattered our silent vigil. With two tears rolling slowly down her cheeks, Aniela began to recite the prayer for the dead: "Eternal rest give unto them, O Lord, and let perpetual light shine upon them . . .'

On 15 September, they operated on another girl from our transport. Krysia Dąbska had both legs in plaster after a bone operation. That meant yet another one lying in bed immobilised for several months.

On 16 September they took six more. This time the selection followed a pattern: it was the girls who'd already been injected with bacteria once and who had the same number on their plaster casts: Jadzia Kamińska, Dziunia Karolewska, Urszula Karwacka, all three of whom were still in the rewir recovering from their first operation. The other three were taken from our original group: Wanda Kulczyk, Rózia Gutek and Maria Zielonkowa. Their legs were cut open in the same place as before, and most probably re-infected. But this time they were given letters not numbers.

On 17 September they took Zosia Stefaniak for a second bone operation, and once again throughout the evening and all that night the sound of stifled groans filled the air.

The bone operations were not accompanied by high temperatures, but they were excruciatingly painful. What they probably did was take away the fibrous membrane surrounding the bones. [We now know that they excised the fibula as well as the tibia.] They took away the tibia from one of Zosia's legs, and only two stumps remained, easily visible under X-ray. She would be crippled for life.

On 24 September it was Dziuba Sokulska's turn, but the operation performed on her had nothing to do with either bacteria-injection or bones. It seemed to be a relatively mild affair, just an operation on one leg, and no subsequent temperature. A couple of weeks later, when she was learning to walk again, they operated a second time. Once again there was no contamination with bacteria. Very probably it was a muscle operation.

Six days later they took ten women from the evening roll-call. At that time there were no lights in the camp at night, and they simply disappeared into the darkness – no one knew where. We were certain that they were going to be executed; and it was not till next morning that we heard they were lying in the rewir waiting to be operated on.

Sometimes we wondered which was preferable: execution or operation. By now we had all realised that for us there was no other choice: for those in the Special Transports there was only death or experimentation. That these two might be one and the same we had yet to learn.

The ten they had taken that morning were deliberately infected with bacteria, the infection being inserted into an incision in the right leg the whole length of the tibia. (In the case of one girl, it was the left leg.) They too had mysterious letters marked on their white dressings, though their legs were not put in plaster.

They lay, as we had done, delirious with raging fever, and on five consecutive days after the operation they received a 5 cm intra-muscular injection three times a day. (They weren't all given the same injection.) On the fifth day, the injections stopped. Weronika Kraska's condition immediately got worse. She complained of a dreadful numbness in the jaws and a strangely stiff neck.

When Dr Schidlausky was told, he ordered the window to be shut, saying that the stiff neck was due to a draught. As for the numbness in the jaw, he dismissed it as toothache. Until that time, Weronika Kraska (designated E I), a strong, healthy woman, had not known what toothache was.

By evening her condition was worse. She passed a terrible night, and by next day it was clear that she was dying. She knew it herself. She could barely speak, and water had to be poured into her mouth through her tightly clenched teeth. It was lock-jaw – tetanus.

Summoning her last ounce of strength, she managed a few despairing words about her two small children who would now have no one to care for them. The words died away and a harsh rattle was heard in her throat. Her face contorted into a fearsome grimace, and her head twisted awkwardly on the stiffened neck. She was on the point of death.

Sister – the one we called 'Scarlet' – came running in and swiftly and smoothly inserted a needle under Weronika's skin. A little 1 cm injection. When the needle was taken out, it was taken from a corpse. The effect of the injection had been instantaneous.

Kraska's tortured face was horrible to see, but after a

while it softened and became smoother. Under death's gentle touch, she became almost beautiful.

Some crow-like German women came and hastily removed the body. They were followed almost immediately by Dr Oberheuser with an injection for Zofia Hoszowska whose serial letter E II was the same as the dead woman's. For ten days Zofia was given those injections.

News of Kraska's death spread through the camp, and our Special Transport understood at last that there was a third possibility open to us: experimentation *and* death. Death by operation or death by execution – in either case, the common denominator was death.

The very same day, they selected a group of twelve women and, as with the previous one, deliberately infected them with bacteria. Twelve hitherto healthy women now writhing in indescribable agony. In their case, long incisions either along the tibia or further back, on the right calf. Twelve more hearts beating in furious rhythm as the fever rose above 40°C. Virulent bacteria rampaging through twelve more healthy bodies and doing their deadly work.

There they lay, twelve of them – all from Lublin – while over the ensuing difficult days the experiment ran its course: high temperature, hearts growing weaker, and pain . . . always pain . . .

Two days after the operation, a further incision was made on the legs of the two women who bore the letter K: Halina Pietrzak – K II – and Fredzia Prusówna – K I. Fredzia began to haemorrhage badly. At first only the bandage was soaked, then the blanket, then the mattress, until finally there was a red pool of blood under the bed. A pretty girl was bleeding to death under the very eyes of her friends. The doctors made a belated, last-minute attempt to save her. Dr Oberheuser injected glucose into her veins and gave her two saline injections. But it was no use. When the other girls begged for Fredzia to be given a blood transfusion, Dr Oberheuser said that they didn't have the necessary equipment. It was true, they didn't.

Death was fast approaching for Fredzia. They took her,

pale as a communion wafer, out of the room; and she died in a smaller, single room in another section.

The death of Fredzia, such a luminous, gentle and popular girl, weighed like a millstone on our hearts.

Nightmare days. The whole camp had begun to regard our Lublin Special Transport with superstitious terror, as befitted those who were under sentence of death. Every day there were fewer of us – our numbers were being steadily reduced by experiment or execution. And practically every week a new contingent was sent to the rewir.

By now there was no one at Ravensbrück who did not know about the experiments being performed on the Special Transport from Lublin and Pawiak. The terrible secret was a secret no longer, but stool-pigeons in the camp began circulating lies about the large sums of money being paid to our families as compensation.

Aniela Lefanowicz was the third girl to die. It was obvious right from the start that she was not going to pull through. After the operation she couldn't move, couldn't even sit on a bedpan. After a few days they took her away, as they had taken Fredzia. And, like Fredzia, she died.

Shortly afterwards, Zofia Kiecolowa from Chełmno died, this time from heart-failure, induced by drugs and raging fever.

Next to go was Kazia Kurowska. Her death was not like the others. She was a strong, healthy young country-girl whose heart was as sound as a bell. But her legs had been injected with bacteria. Grey, almost black, swollen to four times their natural size, Kazia's legs were the cause of her death. Her strong young heart did not want to give in, and for several days she fought bravely for her life. But she too died.

In a few short days, we had lost five women who had so recently been in good health. The shadow of their deaths struck chill into mind and body, and all of us, whether or not we had yet been operated on, found it harder to go on living. Terror had entered our barbed-wire compound and held us in an unrelenting grip. We could no longer find the courage to smile or to sing. We couldn't even cry.

14

Herded together and driven to work like cattle, adrift among hostile strangers, we were young women without a future. Things were so bad now, it was hard to see how they could possibly get worse. And yet every day brought news of fresh calamities.

There were large numbers in the rewir now. The 'bone' people continued to lie in their single rooms, while the bacteria victims returned to their blocks after about two months.

"The guinea-pigs are increasing and multiplying," we said, in an occasional burst of black humour.

In this way, the number of cripples rapidly increased. Basia Pietrzyk, the baby of our transport, was taken on her own. A graceful girl, hardly more than a child, who adored dancing and was life and movement personified. At home, she used to go to ballet school where her dark hair and black eyes had earned her the nickname 'Pepper'.

They took those legs that so loved movement and dancing, and removed a large section of bone from them. Then, for good measure, they injected them with bacteria. She lay there, butchered, her legs in plaster – still trying to smile.

The second youngest was Staszka Sledziejowska, gay, wild 'Sledzia' who couldn't stay still for two minutes at a time, yet who was condemned to spend several months in bed after a series of so-called muscle operations. Five times she was operated upon. They made four preliminary incisions, two on her thighs and two on the calves. Then at two-week intervals, they opened up the incisions one after another, probably in order to remove some muscle.

The number of 'guinea-pigs' grew all the time while an idea had gained ground in the camp that these operations were a safeguard against summary execution. When the names of Rózia Gutek and Aniela Okoniewska were deleted from the death-list, this belief was re-inforced. And then something happened which seemed to bear out the rumour still further.

Towards the end of October Aniela Okoniewska was taken to the rewir and, in the presence of the Sister and the nurse, an official from the Political Department read out a statement formally exempting her from the death sentence. He offered no explanations, but he looked at her leg, and everyone automatically concluded that the exemption was connected with the operation; though, of course, we couldn't be sure. Aniela was all smiles again, but some of the women were green with envy. And Aniela did, in fact, survive.

It was not the first time that we had aroused envy, but from now on it became more and more obvious. Starving, frightened women, actually envied us our fate, believing that the experiments performed on us were a guarantee that we would stay alive.

All of us who underwent the operations made it our top priority to ease the lot of the newest 'guinea-pigs'. As soon as they came round, these latest arrivals received advice about the best position to lie in, in order to keep the pain in their legs to a minimum; about which sister was a bitch, and which one was alright. Remembering also how we had gone hungry when fever prevented us from swallowing the revolting and, even at the best of times, unpalatable soup they had offered us, we organised some help from the kitchen. We only managed to do so thanks to the Polish cooks, Kama and Hanka, Joasia Kukulska and all the others who daily put their lives at risk so as to provide a little tea or sugar for the victims.

As a result of the recent spate of deaths, conditions in the rewir began to improve slightly. The girls were now being put on diets (the usual camp rations put through a mincer); and there was a sister on duty at night.

The next twelve victims, and the ten after that, were all from the Lublin transports. Bone experiments and contamination by bacteria. In the case of the second batch, they changed the order of procedure, injecting the bacteria first and operating on the bone twenty-four hours later.

The girls returned from the operating theatre with no incisions, but with what looked like small pin-pricks on the right calf, covered by pieces of sticking plaster. They joked that they'd got off lightly.

And to begin with all was indeed well. But, as night fell, everything changed. It followed the usual pattern: the swollen legs, the angry red swellings growing larger and larger, the characteristic cramps, the soaring temperatures that raged till morning. Next day Dr Oberheuser chose the four whose veins stood out most prominently and began to pump into them a whole battery of injections, both intravenous and intramuscular, several times a day. The remaining women were operated on again. Incisions of different lengths, stretching sometimes from ankle to knee, and of varying widths, some along the tibia, others further back.

After two weeks the four who'd been pumped full of injections were sent back to the block. Obviously the injections had got the better of the sepsis. They returned exhausted, still feverish and in a certain amount of pain, but nevertheless happy that their legs were still in working order. Some of them had a rash of large red lumps, for which they continued to be given injections, even after their return.

Christmas was coming, and the weather was getting much colder. Our weak legs were frozen – our sound ones too, for that matter. We were cold and hungry. And in the rewir lay many sick, weak, and tortured women who every month still penned their lying message home: "I am well and happy."

15

It was the end of December, 1942 was coming to a close and the 'guinea-pigs' went on multiplying. Everyone in the camp now openly called us by that name, and the close-kept secret of this criminal human rights' violation was so well-known that it scarcely aroused comment any longer. We had the sympathy of the entire camp, or at least of the political prisoners within it.

Anonymous strangers who worked outside the camp would run to the rewir window when they returned in the evening and furtively throw inside a bunch of raw carrots, an apple or a tomato. It is no exaggeration to say that hundreds of women risked their lives for us like this.

It was obvious to everyone who had not yet been brutalised by the camp that women who were running a 40 degree temperature needed extra care and special food. The cooks would steal sugar, coffee or buckwheat groats for the 'guinea-pigs' from the SS stores, smuggling the buckwheat kasha into the rewir at every possible opportunity. It was automatically accepted that we, the weakest and most ill-treated of all the women, were the ones in greatest need of care. Those wonderfully noble women regarded it as their sacred duty to look after us and, to the best of their ability, to help those who suffered most.

Every single thing that made our lives more bearable: the leather shoes, sheets, clean underwear, blankets or special foods, we owed to our companions who somehow managed to get them for us. The camp authorities gave us nothing to relieve our suffering, despite many rumours to the contrary. Our block-leader often lied to the overseer, saying that we had 'bed-cards', even when they had been taken away from us. Frequently one of the more articulate Polish women who spoke fluent German would summon up enough gall to inform the store-overseer that we were to have leather shoes, since we were the special leg cases. And because some of the overseers were stupid and incapable of doing us real harm, a fast-talking, self-confident prisoner could often work wonders for us, while we ourselves – old hands in the rewir – could often outwit the new bewildered officials who had been dragged in to look after us. In other words, it was thanks to the co-operation of practically the whole camp – our fellow prisoners – and the stupidity of those in charge, that we had our 'privileges': privileges which meant, however, that we were set apart from the rest as a group.

As the months and then the years passed, more and more Polish women came to hold leading positions in the camp, despite all the insults hurled at the Polish way of doing things. In the end, even the Germans admitted that the Polish block-leaders were reliable, did not steal and were good at organising the blocks. From our point of view, it was a great help to have this growing number of our compatriots as block-leaders. But it wasn't only the Poles who helped us. Whenever I think about the 'guinea-pigs', I am irresistibly reminded of the Czech girl, Marzena Svedikowa.

At the end of October 1942, a general stock-taking roll-call had taken place. Weighed down with all our possessions, we stood there the whole day long, until eventually the Germans made one of those serious blunders which may possibly have saved our lives. They went back to grouping us by nationality and in numerical order and on that basis assigned us to new blocks. So we were all together again in block 15, and our new block-leader was the Czech, Marzena Svedikowa, shrewd, brave and very, very kind. Block 15 represented our first real change for the better.

The second improvement came in December 1942, when our families were allowed to send food parcels. A few arrived in time for Christmas, and for the first time for many months we stopped being hungry. We had a bit of sugar, and more importantly, were able to take better care of our invalids.

It was an emotional occasion, the arrival of those first parcels, and we queued for hours in the cold to get them. Though we later protested that we were not in the least emotionally affected, we would furtively cut out the address-panel which had been written by a dearly-loved hand. Sometimes, at the sight of a box from home carefully packed with goodies and little trinkets, we had to choke back the tears. Longings returned to devour us, passionate and full of pain.

In block 15, a distinct and rather unusual grouping of young people began to emerge, and it was this group that now staged a revolt on a specific issue, the first in the history of the camp. (Later on, we would become notorious, which was why the Germans called us 'the bandit block'.)

From time to time the Germans used to pick out prisoners for the 'puf' – the soldiers' brothel, and those who agreed to go there were given their release from the camp. Usually it was the professional prostitutes (the 'black triangles') to whom these propositions were made. But one day our Polish blocks were summoned to HQ, where an overseer invited us to volunteer for the serving soldiers' 'puf'. In all the Polish transports from Lublin and Pawiak, there wasn't a single 'black triangle' – the prostitutes had all been left behind in the Castle, and only the politicals had been despatched to the camp.

When the overseer had finished, there was a thunderous silence. After a time, one girl did step forward (she was a professional prostitute who somehow had been given a red, political prisoner's triangle) and a storm of boos greeted her. Everyone was fuming. For the first time, we felt so enraged that we didn't give a damn about endangering our lives. We sent a group of delegates to the camp commandant, with the polite request that never again should such a proposition be put to Polish prisoners. It was an affront to our feminine self-respect, we told him, we were not prostitutes but political prisoners, and would the Herr Kommandant please remember it.

The commandant gaped at us, and hadn't the slightest idea what to say or do. Only after a lengthy silence did he pull himself together enough to ask us which block we were from.

As a punishment, we were forbidden to have letters or parcels for two weeks – this at a time when the number of parcels had reached its peak – and our spokeswoman, Jadzia K., was arrested.

We fairly trembled with indignation. At first the Germans tried pointedly to distribute our parcels to other prisoners; but the whole camp responded by showing its solidarity with us. Nobody would accept the parcels that were meant for us. In the end, they gave them to some gypsies who had only recently arrived in the camp and had no idea what was going on.

But the incident drove the first wedge between young and old in our block. Two weeks without food parcels was indeed a cruel punishment since it condemned us to fourteen long days of hunger. Other women who went out to work in the fields could supplement their diet with what they found there; but we of the Special Transport were not allowed to leave the camp compound. As a result, one of the older women complained that because of the fuss we'd made, *they* would have to go hungry, through no fault of their own. A cheeky youngster replied that indeed it wasn't any fault of theirs, since the offer had not been for the likes of them; they were twenty years too old for the profession in question.

A nasty situation was in the making, and several more insults flew around. The atmosphere was so unpleasant that Pelusia burst into tears. I couldn't help saying to the woman who was shouting the loudest and who had a daughter of my own age back home: "Well, madam, I just hope they persuade your daughter to do what you're trying to get us to do." That shut her up.

Fortunately not all the older women were against us. Mrs Chorążyna said a few conciliatory words, and the storm began to abate. But it left behind a sour after-taste, and not a little bitterness, even though Polish girls were never again asked to put their names down for the brothel. Our trust in older women was shattered. We began to revise our earlier attitudes. Against our will, we found ourselves forced to keep a wary eye on each other, and particularly on those women whose grey hairs had hitherto commanded our deepest respect.

So it had been a pyrrhic victory and the antagonism between the generations was there to stay. I don't remember exactly when we realised that the older ones were trying to get us to do their work. We didn't argue about it; on the contrary, we tried to spare our grey-haired colleagues as much as we could. But sometimes their strength was greater than ours. Young girls faded more rapidly than full-grown adult women, and in time the cooking-pots became just as difficult for us as for them. We were willing to help each other – and them – but some made it quite plain that it was our bounden duty to do so. Hunger often drove people to do terrible, mean-spirited things.

I remember one kindly, grey-haired woman, a teacher by profession . . . I had often seen her, because we sat quite near to each other. One midday, while I was still post-operative and therefore able to stay behind in the block during roll-calls, I saw something so unbelievable that I could scarcely trust the evidence of my own eyes. Through the half-open door of the dining-room, I saw our silver-haired lady peeling potatoes for the entire block. From each plateful she took a potato and hid it in a sack. When she left carrying the sack, I followed her, as though drawn by a magnet. I thought that she was perhaps taking it to the rewir for a sick friend. But no. She went to the latrine and I followed her in, spying on someone for the first time in my life. She wasn't expecting to be overlooked and immediately began to wolf down all the raw potatoes. I climbed down from my perch and walked away, sick at heart and with a deep sense of betrayal. I told no one, and was careful to behave no differently to the woman in question. But the incident affected me badly, and since that moment I have never respected anybody, neither man nor woman, for the sake of their grey hairs alone.

I sobbed like a child that night, and Krysia was terrified for me even though as a rule it no longer surprised us to see a woman weep. Time was teaching us to grow hard. We did not weep at roll-call when the rifle shots rang out, though we knew very well what they signified. We did not weep when the death-lists were delivered to the block and we learned the names of those who would be killed next day. The condemned women did not weep as they walked away – no, never once – and neither did we who were left behind. For us there was only silence.

How terrible is the silence of a crowd of women! There are so many kinds of silence, more than the imagination can grasp! For example the sudden silence as an expression of fear, when packs of SS men and women with dogs and whips encircled our rows of helpless women, waiting for the signal to attack. It may seem fanciful to describe a silence as being deep or hard. But we were also familiar with silence in all its unbelievable expressiveness. Words may be eloquent, but how much more so is silence, especially the silence of many thousands of people. Roll-calls, when they took people out of the line and executed them, cloaked us in a seamless silence at the heart of which was something far deeper than fear. There was no longer any fear when we faced the shadow of death.

So 1942 drew finally to a close. The last months of that year saw the beginnings of what later became a close-knit clan: the group of younger 'guinea-pigs'. It was the time too of growing conflict between young and old; but I must admit that there were older women who always showed us great kindness precisely because of our 'lost youth'. Mother Liberakowa, still to this day remembered as 'mother' by all the 'guinea-pigs', was unfailingly supportive, as were Halina Chorążyna, Mrs Stefa and many others. There is no doubt that we aroused the maternal instincts of these women and they protected us to the best of their ability, not only from other elderly women but even sometimes from each other. We were schooled by the camp, but we learned something too from these older companions of ours who gave us the best that was in them.

What a nightmarish year 1942 had been! And the future was no more hopeful. Our hearts were full of dread as we wondered what 1943 might have in store for us.

16

1943 came in, grey and depressing. Nothing much changed in January although the sufferers in the rewir were now slowly recovering their strength. When we demanded to know why these operations were being performed on us, the doctors would inevitably fob us off with silly bantering replies: "Oh, it's because there are such gorgeous women in your transport." When we asked the commandant, he said he didn't know anything about any operations, and we'd have to ask the doctor. It was no use.

Our friends continued to be taken to the rewir. We counted up: seventy-one of us had been operated on, and sixty-six were still alive. Sixty-six women with an uncertain future, haunted by thoughts of death and disablement. The 'bone' cases doubted whether they would be able to walk again, while most of the 'injectees' knew that their legs would never return to normal. Their wounds were healing and scars were forming, but they never knew just how and when the bacteria injected into their veins might revive.

In block 15 we were surrounded by kindness and lived in relative comfort. Mama Liberakowa did everything in her power to make the 'guinea-pigs'' lives easier to bear. Meanwhile in the rewir Dr Oberheuser announced that there would be no more operations. How we longed for that statement to be true.

On the surface things went on much as before, and yet the signs of change were gradually becoming ever more apparent. We had less hesitation now in declaring that we'd had enough. Perhaps it was just that our normal reactions were beginning to re-assert themselves. The zombie-like, famished wrecks, now somewhat fortified thanks to food parcels, were becoming human beings once again.

The air was thick with growing tension. The sight of so many disabled people in the one block (even those of us who are once again mobile today were still crippled at this time), had its effect on us, making us aware of ourselves as a cohesive group. No longer were we lost and abandoned in a crowd of hostile women; we were discovering a mysterious and growing sense of our own power.

On 10 February 1943, eight women from the Warsaw transport, including one victim of medical experimentation, were led out to execution. Next day it was the turn of a group from our Lublin transport: among those shot was Marysia Gnaś, who had been operated on in the rewir.

Every day now, more executions; more women led away to their deaths.

Block 15 was in a ferment. In the past we had waited in gloomy silence for whatever was about to happen. But this new bout of executions awoke a frantic anxiety in us, and made it abundantly clear that far from the operations being a guarantee against death, one could be experimented on five times over and still have to face a firing squad.

It was these tragic events that drove us to a new determination: to act, to do something, to counter our own helplessness.

On one of the many sleepless nights, Nina stumbled on the idea, outrageous in its simplicity, that we should alert the people at home to what was happening in Ravensbrück. With fluttering hearts we prepared to put this plan into operation, and try to make contact with Lublin. From now on we had a goal: to let the outside world know what was being done in the camp. This dangerous game, played out at the very centre of a German camp, exhilarated us and enabled us to climb out of the pit of despair. We would find it easier to die if we could be certain that news of our deaths would reach the world outside.

We waited for confirmation – for the red thread concealed in a parcel, which would be the sign that our information had been received. And all the while the storm clouds around us were gathering force.

It was rumoured – and the story was barely believable – that one woman had tried to run away just before her execution. This woman, the sister-in-law of our own dead Maryśia Gnaś, was of very striking appearance, with huge, dark eyes. Somehow or other she had got over the wall and walked in her striped dress into the fields beyond. She was caught, of course, and hauled before the commandant. Questioned as to how she'd got over the wall, she replied that she had been 'in a trance'. And indeed, when one looked into those huge, black eyes, the idea did not seem all that far-fetched. As to why she had run away, she replied that she had not much liked the idea of being shot.

We tried to discover how she had got over that wall, obsessed by the fact that she had indisputably done so, and that if she could do it, so could we. But the wall was as straight and smooth as ever and the electrified wires had not been displaced. At no point was there the slightest possibility of getting through. Our imaginations worked overtime. Gone was our zombie-like spinelessness. As a mute determination to resist grew in us, our backs stiffened and a kind of suicidal courage possessed our souls.

Feelings were running high; fights, quarrels and disagreements now filled our days. The climax came when someone or other hurled a cruelly mindless accusation at us 'guinea-pigs': "You lot went off without a protest, just like sheep. You might as well have been volunteers." The thrust went home and cut us to the quick. At the time of the operations, the sheer humiliation of being used as guinea-pigs had sent a shudder through us all, and every one of us had contemplated the possibility of refusal. But we were powerless, since they always tricked us into believing that we were going to the doctor or to the labour market, or even to the execution ground. We had never known exactly where they were taking us.

Yes, we had been utterly powerless then. But the sense of powerlessness had long tormented us, and now we were determined to be rid of it. Enough of experiments, of lies, of trickery. We had gritted our teeth and gone wherever they had taken us, just as we had kept silent when they struck us in the face, knowing that to retaliate would invite further punishment and possibly death.

We had endured the operations because we had been given no choice. But the murder of two of our number had put a powerful weapon into our hands: the suicidal courage of people who could act as they chose today because they knew that by tomorrow they would be dead. We now openly voiced the thought that we had earlier pushed to the backs of our minds: the Germans were bound to finish by killing us because it stood to reason that they would not allow such 'living proofs' of their activities to remain alive. We were, after all, a considerable blot on the conscience of the Third Reich. Wordlessly, we all reached the same conclusion at the same moment: enough was enough.

The first girl to act on this new determination was Dziuba Sokulska. On 13 March she was sent for to the rewir, and refused to go. They took her to the commandant. She repeated her refusal, adding that she knew perfectly well what was intended; they had already operated on her twice, and she was not going to stand for it a third time.

The commandant seems to have been at a loss, since he merely asked if she understood the consequences of her action.

She returned to the block and we all hailed this first resounding "No!" with enthusiasm. How we loved Dziuba for that courageous: "I won't go!"

That afternoon, Zosia Stefaniak, one of several women who'd previously been operated on and were now awaiting further experiments, jumped out of the rewir window and returned to the block. Zofia Modrowska was summoned (for a second time) and refused to go. The whole block throbbed with returning life: we were doing something at long last. At long last we could feel that we were human again.

Next morning a new list arrived. Five women were to present themselves at the rewir. With one voice they said "No". Instead they would go and see the commandant. We sat down and prepared a 'petition' for them to take with them. Mrs Chorążyna drew it up as we clustered round her, flushed with excitement. In a few brief sentences we stated that we, the undersigned political prisoners, wished to know whether the commandant was aware that experiments were being performed on completely healthy women in his camp – all of them political prisoners. We stated that these experiments had led to maiming and even death – here we gave the names of those who had died as a result of the experiments; that international law forbade experiments on human beings without their consent; and that we, the victims, hereby registered a formal protest against such experiments.

We all signed the petition. For the record, I must admit that a few signatures were missing. But this fact was basically unimportant, since any consequences would automatically fall on the whole group; and in any case the authorities would probably not even notice the absence of one or two signatures.

We were perfectly well aware of what the consequences might be, but we didn't care. To be honest, we didn't really expect that our protest would yield any positive result, nor did we suppose that it would affect the course of the experiments already in progress. What mattered most was that we could be seen to be making a stand. For too long we had provided living proof of our own powerlessness and passivity.

We went in rows of four to see the commandant. There were about fifty from our block, all of us limping; some of us carrying the weakest ones in our arms. Some were on crutches . . . We must have been a grotesque sight. Women passing us in the camp street gave us terrified glances. The rest of the camp was unaware of what we were doing.

It was a lovely sunny day. Slowly, one step at a time, our little procession made its way forward. It was the first time we had been out all together – we still had 'bed-cards' and exemption from roll-calls. Our white bandages stood out starkly against the black coal-dust of the street. Hobbling, hopping, struggling with wooden crutches, we were a disorderly and motley parade. There were some healthy ones among us – girls who had just received their first summons to the rewir – and they carried the most enfeebled in their arms.

It seemed a dauntingly long way to the main office block, but we eventually arrived at the building which housed the commandant's office. Beneath the windows the flame-coloured salvias were in flower, their colour seeming more strident than ever against our white-bandaged legs. Not that by this time our bandages were all that white – for most of us the march had been beyond our puny strength, and a yellowish-green discharge mixed with blood was seeping through our dressings.

The commandant did not deign to appear. He sent a woman clerk to tell us that all this talk of operations and experiments was the product of hysterical women's over-heated imaginations; everyone knew that women were taken to the rewir just to have their temperatures taken three times a day – nothing more. We were to be good girls and go back to the block.

The woman clerk spoke without much conviction. After all, it must have been difficult to speak of 'hysterical' imaginings when faced with those scores of bandaged legs. But we took her up on her own words, retorting that if it was only a matter of taking temperatures then it was immaterial which women were selected; and the next batch certainly didn't have to be the five from our transport. There was no denying the logic of this, and that very day, as if to back up his assertion, the commandant sent messengers round to all the blocks, asking for volunteers to present themselves three times a day at the rewir in order to have their temperatures taken. Naturally there were no volunteers, though the invitation was sent to every block in the camp.

Marzena, who had gone along with us as interpreter when we went to see the commandant, triumphantly read us the invitation during the evening roll-call.

We'd won that round. The five intended victims had

been saved, at least for the moment. They were not sent for that day, nor the next. In fact, they were not sent for at all, and their legs remained strong and healthy. We never discovered whether it was as a result of our protest that no more women were taken to the rewir, or whether outside developments had affected the issue. All that mattered was that the experiments were now at an end.

Our little demonstration of defiance had increased our self-confidence. The commandant steered clear of us. The whole affair was hushed up, and we were visited by none of those dire consequences which the more timorous women in our block had foretold. They had tried to persuade us to go on agreeing to the operations, so as not to endanger the lives of everyone else.

We didn't go entirely unpunished, however. After a cursory inspection of our legs, we were deprived of our diet-sheets and bed-cards and ordered back to work. Only the completely bedridden were allowed to remain behind in the block, though many of us were still badly crippled and all of us had either open wounds or fresh scars which were liable to open up again at the least movement.

So once again, we had to stand for the labour roll-call with the rest of the 'floaters' – the name given to prisoners without a regular job. We stood in that 'market-place', a huge polyglot crowd of women, while groups of overseers pranced round us, eager to snap up this free work-force. We were grabbed by a German woman and put in an 'unloading' unit. They drove us through the gate to the lake, where a boat laden with rocks was moored. We had the job of unloading the rocks on to a lorry which stood by the lakeside. At first it wasn't too awful: the topmost stones were fairly small, and the empty lorry was not too high for us. But as the number of stones on the boat decreased, it became correspondingly harder to throw them over the ship's side and on to the lorry. We filled one vehicle, then a second, and so on until we reached ten. Tensing our muscles, we swung those massive blocks of stone backwards and forwards in order to gather sufficient momentum to hurl them on to the bank. As often as not, they would fall with a crash back to the bottom of the boat, bruising our feet as they fell, and scraping our damaged legs with their sharp edges.

At first we made light of it, joking that the exercise was good for us after so many months of lying in bed. But the laughter soon stopped, and our hearts, weakened from drugs, pain and morphine, began to pound madly in our breasts. We were quite literally collapsing from exhaustion. One girl actually did faint, and we carried her in our arms back to the camp. We were all unimaginably exhausted.

Not everyone was put to unloading stones. Some had been seconded to other kinds of work, but in one respect it was the same: an opportunity for spreading propaganda. Our legs were stockingless, and our bandages or fresh blue-black scars were easily visible even at a distance. We aroused universal interest. One of our girls told a Czech driver about the operations, another spoke to some French women about them, and a third told a newly-arrived young overseer. As a result, an order came through next morning that on no account were the medical experiment cases to leave the confines of the camp; they were to work only indoors.

After that they got us to knit stockings as part of a large work-unit of elderly or unfit women. For lack of a proper workroom, we worked in the dining-room of our block. Our production target was one pair of stockings per week, and the work was pleasant in that we could sit in our own surroundings without an overseer being present. The other knitters did everything possible to distract us from the ghastly boredom of the actual work. Mrs Peretiatkowicz would tell us about the earth and its geological or geographical marvels: and Mrs Chorążyna lectured us on chemistry. We persuaded Mrs Tyrankiewicz to teach us something, too, and, depending on the mood she was in, she would talk about animal psychology, or discourse on the subject of Polish literature.

Since the day we had made our protest we had improved in appearance and temper. Our behaviour was different now. We laughed aloud, sang songs; and when we were told definitely that they were going to kill us, we argued about whether the smoke from 'Jim' would be red, by virtue of his well-known 'temperament', or whether perhaps Stenka would turn it yellow. We argued passionately about marriage and children, and the very young women would turn and look in 'Jim's' direction whenever anyone deprecated motherhood as an over-rated occupation: "Children? Who wants them? Noise and filthy nappies all day long, ugh, dreadful." The youngsters would get so het up that they would have liked to have given birth on the spot in protest, just to be able to prove their contention that motherhood was to be the sole aim and purpose of their lives. We no longer worried about death, but we kept on pretending to persuade 'Jim' that motherhood, not death, was a woman's true calling.

We nearly killed ourselves laughing when the 'G Club' began their secret meetings. Its members were confirmed and incorrigible smokers who were convinced that no one could either see or hear them. They issued invitations to each other in loud stage whispers to meet 'in the loft'. To get there, they had to stand on a third-tier bunk, lever two planks from the ceiling and squeeze themselves upwards through the resultant gap. The planks creaked unmercifully when the whole 'club' was up there.

God knows where they got their cigarettes from. We hazarded various guesses about their composition, but as there was nothing else really available, they could only have been smoking straw from their mattresses. We never found out for sure, but whatever it was, the smoke was anything but fragrant.

The 'anti-guinea-pig' brigade of older women began to say that we were spoiled brats. But they were wrong. It's true that at times we were over-rowdy, but often the noise was intended to keep at bay the questions that nagged at us still; what were they going to do to us? would they ever let us go home? and, if we did return, would it be with our legs permanently crippled? Nothing we did could ever really banish the gnawing fear that such questions rekindled.

17

Block 15 was unbearably overcrowded, but the fact that we had managed to make contact with the outside world was a source of strength to us and helped us to cope. Though we were of such different temperaments and backgrounds, and only a random fate had thrown us together, that same fate had welded us firmly into a single whole, and the links that bound us were strong. By the summer of 1943 we 'guinea-pigs' were a clearly identifiable group. And until 15 August they more or less left us in peace.

We had heard vague reports that they were now using dogs for the experiments, instead of ourselves. But on 15 August* the thunderbolt fell: there were to be more operations in the rewir; the beds and theatre were ready and waiting. We had reliable sources of information inside the rewir, and they contrived to give us advance warning early that morning.

We were in a terrible state . . . Of course we knew that none of us would agree to go; but we had no idea who would be selected or what for. The anxiety was nerve-racking.

In the afternoon a camp policewoman arrived with a list, a piece of white paper signed by someone at the labour office. There were ten names written on it, and the ten were ordered to go straight to the rewir. They refused point blank. The policewoman went away, and we waited anxiously to see what would happen next. We knew the matter wouldn't be allowed to rest.

And before long, the chief overseer Binz came on the

---

* 15 August held a special significance for Wanda Połtawska. As the Feast Day celebrating the Assumption of the Blessed Virgin Mary it is one of the most important Holy Days in the Catholic calendar.

scene with a whole squad of policewomen. They made us all go and stand outside the block and ordered everyone else in the camp to stay indoors. The streets were empty, except for the policewomen posted at the entrance to all the Polish blocks.

The ten were told to come to the front, and Binz tried coaxing them into going to the rewir, giving them her solemn promise that there would be no operations. But we all knew what *her* word was worth.

They were simply wanted for a job, insisted Binz. But we knew all about those six white beds waiting in the rewir.

Finally she lost patience and ordered them to present themselves at headquarters. They said: certainly, they would go there, but not to the rewir. They were taken off under police guard, while the rest of us were pushed and shoved to the far side of the block. We stood there, ten to each row, in deathly silence.

Suddenly from the other side of the wall came the frantic barking of dogs. The whisper that the SS were bringing in the dogs had just gone round when suddenly round the corner came our ten friends, running towards us as fast as their legs would carry them.

Without a word, and as though we had been given a parade-ground order, we opened ranks and shut them again, swallowing up the ten fugitives. In the twinkling of an eye we re-formed so efficiently that when the police-women tore round the corner they saw only the same even ranks as before. But they could read the difference on our faces. Our eyes glinted with a new militancy, and we held our heads high.

Back came Binz, calling out the ten names and numbers. Silence . . . nobody moved a muscle.

"I order you to produce these ten women."

Nobody did so. Nobody so much as reacted. The silence continued.

The official was beside herself with rage; wherever she looked she met only bold, contemptuous stares. Then she hit on an idea. She called out the nastiest policewoman of them all, an old lag with a long criminal record, who knew us all by sight. As this woman pointed to each of the ten in turn, her colleagues dragged them out of the ranks. In the end, all ten were out there in front.

Binz announced that they were all under arrest for disobeying orders and were to go to the prison Bunker. Yes, they agreed, they would go to the Bunker, but they would not go to the rewir.

The policewomen pranced and leaped all round them as they went off, but could do nothing to quell the shouts from the rest of us who had been left behind: "Keep it up. We're all behind you."

Binz now adopted an air of injured innocence and launched into a long discourse about how much she really valued the Poles in the camp; how well off the Polish women were, much better off than anyone else, as they had all the best jobs. And so on and so forth.

I couldn't help myself interrupting her from the front row:

"And only the lucky Polish women are operated on, and only the lucky Polish women are shot."

She flew at me, screeching with fury, but I wouldn't stop:

"Oh yes, only Polish women are operated on – and there've been seventy-one of them."

This wasn't exactly accurate, since some operations had been performed on women of other nationalities, women who were also mentally ill.

"What's this, a mutiny?" she bawled at me.

"No, just the simple truth."

She lifted her hand as if to strike me. I stared at her stonily – as did everyone else – with anger and contempt. For a moment I wondered if she really was going to hit me, but she apparently thought better of it. She grabbed my arm, and I suddenly realised I was not wearing my prison number. Normally that in itself would have merited instant retribution, but Binz was so furious she didn't even notice. I told her my number – 7709 – and she wrote it down, shouting that she would report me to the commandant. She led away our ten friends to the Bunker and ordered us to go back to the block and stay there.

A little later I was taken to the commandant with Jadźka K. and Marzena who came along to interpret.

"Prisoner-in-charge, number 7709 reporting."

The commandant stood in front of me, or rather, towered above me, since he was a giant of a man. He ordered me to repeat what I'd told Binz, and I replied that I had uttered only one sentence, one perfectly true sentence, which I proceeded to translate into German for him.

"And what did you shout out to the women who were going to the Bunker?"

"I asked if they had taken their sweaters, because it would be cold in the Bunker."

That bore no relation to the truth, but the commandant wasn't bothered about that.

Binz could no longer contain herself. She broke in to tell him about the expression on my face when I had spoken that one truthful sentence, how my fists were clenched and my eyes so full of hate that I looked as if I might have killed her. She paused for breath, positively choking with spleen. The commandant examined his fingernails carefully: he was trying to work out what punishment he could give a prisoner for looking at an overseer as if she'd like to kill her.

He came so close that his face was actually touching mine, and bending down he whispered fiercely:

"You know you're all in my power, don't you? You know that if I want to I can call up thirty SS men with machine-guns, and then there wouldn't be so much as an eye or an ear left of any of you in that blasted block 15."

His voice rose to a shout and a spasm of anger contorted his face. I began to feel alarmed. The commandant had a massive bull neck and huge fists, and he was fond of beating people up.

He went on glowering at me, screaming on and on about 'blasted block 15', and suddenly I knew a kind of joy. Block 15 had obviously got under his skin, and all his efforts to break down the Polish transports had come to nothing. Good old block 15! I almost grinned with a childish glee.

He stopped shouting, spluttered a bit, and then spoke more calmly:

"Go back to your block and tell them what I've said."

We went back, but before we'd so much as opened our mouths, the commandant and chief overseer Binz arrived, and an incredible scene took place.

There we were, in the dining-room, making a great din. The block-leader shouted "Achtung," as they entered, and there was instant silence. Nobody stood up. The commandant moved to the middle of the room and said:

"In view of the mutiny that has taken place, I have no alternative but to sentence block 15 to three days house-arrest without food or air." He studied the fingernails on his right hand as he spoke.

A voice came from the crowd:

"It wasn't a mutiny. We just don't want to be experimented on, that's all."

Others joined in:

"Are you aware that it's against international law to experiment on human beings without their permission?"

" – that we're all maimed?"

" – that we were perfectly healthy beforehand?"

" – that five of us died?"

We all chimed in, some in German, some in Polish, while Marzena did an instant translation of the Polish contributions into German. It was the first time in the history of the camp that long-term prisoners had dared to face the commandant with the truth.

He recoiled a step and spoke uncertainly:

"I'm only an SS man and my instructions are to keep order in the camp."

I noticed that by way of a change he was now studying the nails on his *left* hand.

The pair of them withdrew, and within minutes of their departure, a horde of policewomen descended on us. They made us stand in front of the block while they carried out a search, or, more accurately, while they purloined everything they could find. They confiscated anything remotely edible, then drove us back inside, locking the doors and closing the shutters on us. SS men with guns stood at the door. At once it became dark and airless, despite the narrow strips of light which penetrated the few cracks to have escaped the policewomen's notice.

'Grandpa' (one of the older women in our group) immediately took charge of the situation: "Don't shout, don't walk about; make as little movement as possible and conserve your energy." But the air got more and more fetid. We were three hundred women locked inside on a stiflingly hot summer's day and on the third tier of bunks the heat was intolerable.

One enterprising girl, Manicha, tried to push a wooden clog between the window and the shutter. But she couldn't quite manage it, and an SS man cursed her and sent the clog flying with the butt end of his rifle. We continued to sit there in silence.

That evening, at roll-call, there was a glaring gap in the serried ranks of women, marking the absence of block 15. That empty space was propaganda for us, as many thousands of women of different nationalities began asking what had happened to block 15. Before long the whole camp knew that the Polish girls had refused to be subjected to any more operations.

Next day the news was spread even further. There were several women in our block who usually worked in the offices or outside the camp. When the work units went out, their leaders made excuses for the absentees and did not hesitate to explain what had happened to them. The news was taken outside the walls of the camp, and an old gardener, usually renowned for his stinginess, sent us a handful of fruit.

That evening, a group of women crept up to the block, risking the SS bullets to bring us some packets of food. They stole up silently from the opposite end of the camp, opened the shutters quickly but somewhat less silently, and flung their bundles inside. We didn't know who the women were, nor what nationality. It didn't really matter; the whole camp was solidly behind us.

The next day was intolerable. The sun scorched the roof and a suffocating heat came from the ceiling. We felt more dead than alive. Someone fainted. We were at the end of our endurance.

Towards evening on that second day, Binz looked in on us. No one bothered to call us to attention, no one stood up nor even stirred. Who cared about a chief overseer? If only we had some air . . .

Binz told her henchwomen to open the shutters for ten minutes. When the ten minutes were over, we were in an uproar. Someone passing the window had shouted out: "Girls, they've operated on five of them in the Bunker!" The news was confirmed almost immediately; there was no possible doubt about the matter. Half of our friends had been operated on in a cell in the Bunker.

Impotent rage swamped us. Nothing was left of that fine, brave mood of conscious patriotism in which we had watched our ten friends go to the Bunker. There remained only a blind, cold anger – an overwhelming despair that it had all been for nothing.

All that night we argued the pros and cons, vainly trying to convince ourselves that all we had wanted was to make our point, that we couldn't really have expected anything more.

Silence descended like a pall, heavy and suffocating as a shroud.

"Bloody swine!" Manicha was shaking the shutters violently, forcing them apart, hammering at them. Soon she had made a gaping hole into which she triumphantly pushed one of her shoes.

"Misshapen devils, may you never see another day!" she spat, catching sight of a pair of approaching SS legs. Her dark eyes flashed wild and terrible.

We were overwhelmed by grief and fury. What had they done to our friends? Each of us could well remember what it was like just after the operations. Who was there to care for them? Who would bring them water or bedpans? Helplessly we pounded on the wooden walls of the block with our fists.

Up in the loft, in the thin stream of light provided by a tiny window, a tight-lipped Krysia was writing the latest of many illegal letters. Dates, numbers, names. I kept guard. One had to be on one's guard against almost everyone. Only our very closest, most trusted friends knew about those letters.

I looked at that white sheet of paper, praying with all my heart: Dear God, let it get through! We used to pray over those little pieces of paper as though they were the most sacred of relics while our friends risked their lives to smuggle them out of the camp, convinced that, whatever the risk, the letters must get through.

Krysia's letter did get through. All of them did.

18

Roll-call three days later was bizarre to say the least. We staggered and limped out on to the square, to be met with a ripple of acknowledgement, of sympathy, and of understanding. The overseer approached, counting heads as she came. I don't know who it was who keeled over first, or even whether she really did faint or just pretended to. Whatever happened, it was catching. Still in our rows of ten, silently, soundlessly, we slid to the ground, to lie in heaps on the black gravel.

The overseer counted our prostrate bodies.

Meanwhile in the Bunker our ten friends had passed a difficult night, five of them in one cell, five in another. All night long the five who had not been operated on battled with themselves – and with their own desire to stay alive. They decided that if the Germans tried to take them to the operating theatre they would kill themselves rather than go. But how? Bogna tested her belt for strength. She was feverishly excited, following in imagination the scene that would take place next day: "In the morning they'll open the door, and when they come in they'll find five corpses," she said, eyes glistening with excitement. "It really would be something. Come on, girls, this is our moment of truth. We've got to act."

But, as she turned and looked into the eyes of her friends, she knew there would be no corpses next morning. They would go off yet again like so many sheep. They had all sworn that they would rather kill themselves than submit, but Bogna did not believe them. She looked at Dziuba's flushed, brave face. Sure, Dziuba could bring herself to do it, maybe Zośka could too. But Pola? Urszula? Yet perhaps, when the moment came, they would all somehow find enough strength . . . Bogna closed her eyes. Perhaps after all, there would be five corpses. That would give them something to think about, they could hardly operate on corpses. "It would really be a sight for sore eyes," she mused, as she dropped off to sleep. "If only we could be there to see their faces."

Next morning, an overseer came and took Urszula away. She put up a fight, but her fierce, stubborn resistance was broken by a single sentence from the overseer: "If you don't come with me, we shall leave your friends to die."

Urszula understood German, and she allowed herself to be led away. She was taken to the cell where yesterday's victims lay on five bunks, and was told to look after them.

Their plight was pitiful. Major bone operations on both legs. But dreadful though their physical agony was, their mental anguish was infinitely worse. In spite of the resistance they had put up, in spite of their brave show of spirit, their desperate defiance, they had been taken. Yesterday, they had been healthy young women – and now they had been butchered.

Dziunia spoke in a whisper of how the SS had held her arms and legs and stuffed a gag in her mouth. Joanna kept on repeating, over and over again: "My legs, they are so very dirty." They lay there, racked with pain and isolated from the world, while Urszula tiptoed in and out, trying to ease their sufferings.

News of the operations, the unhygienic conditions in which they'd been carried out, and the girls' desperate struggle to save themselves, spread throughout the Bunker and beyond the camp. Everyone came to know about Hela's leg, for example, how such a huge piece of bone had been cut from it that many weeks later, when she tried to stand, the leg simply snapped. They learned about Halina, who had developed a serious skin disease after being discharged with only a flimsy piece of gauze over her leg as a dressing. And they learned about the butchery performed on Stefa and Joanna.

It was the 'shopping commando' who spread the news

furthest afield – the work-unit which went out to Neustre-litz to get the bread rations for the camp – to the Polish boys in a prisoner-of-war camp there.

It's a mystery why the authorities didn't foresee what was likely to happen: it only needed one visit from a Polish work-unit for contact to be established. But the overseers couldn't understand why there was never any shortage of volunteers for this really rather unpleasant job. They never guessed the attraction it held for us. It was well worth humping heavy sacks about, if once or twice a week we could get to Neustrelitz.

It began with the innocent whistling of a Polish folk-tune followed by a few hastily exchanged words. Everything else followed. A little quiet smuggling took place, becoming more daring and bare-faced as time went on. The boys gave us soap, chocolate, cigarettes and raisins, and in return we stole some wool, dyed it with chemicals pilfered from the rewir, and produced large quantities of gloves, ear-muffs and socks for them. The 'shopping commando' were incredibly slick in making the deliveries. God alone knows how they managed it, since they always had to pass the guard and be searched. It may have been easy enough to conceal lightweight woollen socks, but how on earth did they hide 'The Legend Of Young Poland' or a volume of the collected works of Mickiewicz?

The first time we saw a Polish book, after so many months of being deprived, was an unforgettable experi-ence. When *Pan Tadeusz* arrived, Mrs Saint began to read it aloud to us, and we 'guinea-pigs' just sat there in a tremulous silence. You only get silence of that sort when tears are just below the surface, pricking at the eyelids. Others, less hardened than us, were sobbing openly. Women who, before long, would smile and sing on their way to death, now wept broken-heartedly as they listened to the well-known verses.

Our contact with the boys obsessed us; and as we weren't allowed out ourselves we did what we could to keep it going strong. They were our route to the outside world; it was 'our boys' who sent off those precious secret letters containing chapter and verse about the goings-on in the camp.

We became very attached to 'our boys', though we knew nothing about them. Let's face it, we were in love, and later on, when the time of liberation was in sight, we were all madly embroidering eagles for them. We got the crazy idea that by hook or by crook we'd get some red and white thread and embroider eagles for the boys, and we did it, though I'm sure they never had any idea to what dangers those emblems had exposed us.

Halfway through September, we discovered that there was a French priest in the prisoner-of-war camp; and then our secret smuggling reached new heights of audacity. White wafer discs were smuggled out to us in a little tin box marked 'Sanctissimum'.

On that occasion, there was something profoundly holy about the silence of block 15. We posted look-outs at all the windows, while a long line of women threaded their way through the rows of beds to receive a crumb of white wafer. Back on my top bunk, I looked down at their faces, rapt, solemn, at times radiant. For some it was a living miracle, and others, their own hearts thudding with fear, envied them their calm. And there were a few who stood aside, watching in uncomprehending silence. The prayers poured out in a fervent whisper: give peace to our troubled souls. No one profaned the sacred moment.

A few days later, on 23 September, the executions began again. Four of the 'guinea-pigs' were taken and shot. Pela Rakowska bade us goodbye with a quiet smile on her face. "God be with you," she said calmly, "I am going to rejoin my son." I watched her as she went; she had the same radiant smile, the same steadiness of eye, as when she had received the communion wafer. As she left, she made the sign of the Cross over the block, blessing those of us who were staying behind on this side of death. On this side? Was there anyone among us who did not wonder: for how much longer?

With Pela went nineteen-year-old Rózia Gutek who had once before been given a last-minute reprieve; and Marysia

Zielonkowa, mother of two children whom she had had to leave behind when she was taken from her cottage. We went on staring after them, too choked to speak. Four blood-stained dresses came back to the laundry. Flames from the crematorium chimney lit up the blackness of that night. They had only recently built that brick crematorium, just outside the wall. It was quite a small one, just adequate for the needs of the camp.

We had no doubt that they would shoot us all before the end. Time was on their side, and there were no signs yet of the war coming to an end.

From this certainty a reckless courage was born. What did we have to lose? The policewomen left us alone; these days they didn't strike a 'guinea-pig'. We didn't care one way or the other. Little by little we had come to believe that we were rather special. The more closely fate drove us together, the deeper yawned the gulf that separated us from everyone else. Deep down we resented the fact that we weren't just ordinary, run-of-the-mill prisoners who would almost certainly get out of this place alive. But behind the bitterness lurked a fierce, almost joyful resolve: that as long as we stayed alive, we would at least make our presence felt!

Our arrogance became legendary. And yet, at night, when no one could see us, we wondered frantically what we could do to save ourselves. So desperately did we want to go on living. Whether in the lonely silence of night, or in the more vocal companionship of the day, each one of us was locked into her own struggle against the hopelessness we all felt in the face of approaching death. What strange companions our conflicting emotions made.

"Hey there! 'Soap-cakes!'" shouted Bogna. "Go and have a bath before they turn you into soap!"

'Soap-cakes' rather appealed to us as a name. The youngest ones in particular used to tease Bogna that *they* would make excellent soap, whereas *she* would go up in curling spirals of red smoke, hissing: "We must do something, we must do something." A passionate, sexy smoke, they joked. They laughed and sang, and it wasn't just an act; the laughter was unforced and came from the heart. Nor was it only the young ones who laughed. Even Cissie, once so easily scandalised that we'd nicknamed her 'the priestess', was no longer shocked by our salty jokes. She would burst out laughing and run (if you could call it running) on her mutilated legs, calling out to Marysia, "Hang on a minute, I've got a dirty joke for you." Marysia, who was as squeamish as they come, would stop up her ears and run away as fast as her crutches would allow, while Cissie shouted after her, "It's a really filthy one," to the outrage of all the elderly worthies.

These virtuous ladies were also shocked to find Sledź mimicking 'Dzidzia' coming round after the operation and shouting "Give me my sword!" Bogna laughed at that story till the tears rolled down her cheeks. But others were incensed that we should make a joke out of someone being crippled. They didn't understand that each one of us faced the prospect of becoming a legless cripple, which was why we had to make light of it and turn it into a joke, to belittle the threat.

The older women claimed that we 'guinea-pigs' were all mad; that the operations had sent us round the bend. They said it, for example, when we stood in ranks for hours in the freezing cold, cheerfully humming our favourite slow foxtrot: 'Black Jim's picking cotton', jigging up and down in the cold in a sort of negro dance, trying to revive the circulation in our frozen legs. But the frost bit into our newly-formed scars and we suffered horribly. So we stamped and sang, even though total silence was supposed to be the rule during roll-calls.

It was at this time that the overseers began calling us the 'bandit block'. We were quite the 'in' thing; why else would they spend so much time conducting searches in our quarters? Ever since the London BBC had broadcast a list of names of those who had been medically experimented on, the authorities had been keeping a very wary eye on us. There was even a rumour that we had our own block radio station.

131

We had heard about these broadcasts from some French women who had only recently been brought to the camp. At first sight of our mangled legs, they rubbed their eyes in horrified wonder that any surgeon could have brought himself to do such things. They had heard the broadcasts but had refused to believe them, dismissing the information as mere anti-German propaganda. In this they were not alone. Later on, too, there were many who would not believe, even when confronted by the evidence.

The authorities were furious and left no stone unturned in order to discover how the news had got out. From this time on, our 'bandit block' was continually subject to sudden searches and petty harassment. Flying squads would descend on us at all hours of the day, ordering us to special parades, extra roll-calls and the inevitable searches. At first we nearly had hysterics when the SS women came within inches of finding some of our illicit hoard, but we soon became quite skilled at misleading the search teams, and at inventing ingenious hiding-places for our forbidden treasures.

It was our 'library' that gave us the worst headache. We had amassed about thirty books and didn't want any harm to come to them. Pela, our chief librarian, was worried sick until we finally hit on a safe hiding-place for the books. It was ridiculously simple; we just stuck them underneath the tables and cupboards. The tables had no drawers, and the cupboards had little short feet, and when they were moved, the books moved with them. Somehow it never occurred to anyone to look on the underside of the furniture.

Our confidence grew and sometimes, to the scandal of our companions and the fury of the SS, we could hardly keep our faces straight during these random searches. Once, a particularly nasty overseer dropped in on us, at the very moment when we had managed to acquire twelve calcium glucomate injections for Kawka, at the huge cost of four rations of bread. Kawka had TB and we had had enormous difficulty in getting the calcium for her at all. I had the injections in my hand, when the overseer and her pals rushed in, bawling, "Everybody out." I couldn't think what to do. Hastily, I gave half the injections to Krysia and stowed the remainder in my own pocket. But obviously it was essential to get rid of the things, since at any moment we were going to be individually searched. We walked slowly through the dining-hall. It was dinner-time, and on the table stood a red pot full of turnip soup. The same thought came simultaneously to both of us, and we threw the injections into the soup as we passed. Once outside, we kept the table in our sights as we stood in line, guarding our treasure through the window.

The search went on for ages. We were cold and tired from standing; and I got bored with keeping my eye on that soup-pot. My attention began to wander. Suddenly Krysia touched my hand. I looked at her and saw the corners of her mouth twitching suspiciously. She was obviously trying to keep from laughing, but at first I couldn't imagine what the hilarity was all about. Then I followed the direction of her gaze. Standing by the table, right next to our soup tureen, was a stout, red-faced overseer with a whip in her huge, sweaty paw; while, in the red tureen . . . I had to bite my lip to stop myself laughing out loud. In the red tureen, our injections were jauntily sticking their heads up out of the soup . . . (We wouldn't be able to try that particular dodge again!) Somehow we managed to keep our faces straight and avert our gaze from the bowl, but when the search was over and we were allowed back into the block, we could contain ourselves no longer and laughed till the tears came, much to the bewilderment of our friends. However, at least Kawka got her course of calcium injections and, for a little while at least, her health began to improve.

Even the camp authorities had finally concluded that we were crazy and capable of anything. And to be honest, our outbursts of seeming gaiety were often excessive and bizarre, and in the end even we ourselves began to be afraid of them: for example, we got a sudden, inexplicable urge to burst into song, or to give a defiant rendering of the Marseillaise in the middle of the night. However, the more craven overseers – not to mention the informers and policewomen – began avoiding our block. They no longer dared to strike us. We had won another small victory.

19

The more the camp population had increased, the worse conditions had become: more lice, more scabies, more diseases, more hunger, more death. But we were not concerned only about our physical existence: since it was hopeless to try and protect our bodies, we concentrated our efforts on keeping our spirits alive.

Throughout the autumn of 1943 and the spring of 1944 we ran a school, or rather schools. All our young people were enrolled as students, some with such enthusiasm that on their return home they were allowed to count these studies as part of their university or college courses. The teachers worked with a will, providing courses for various groups of students at all levels. They even provided an anatomy course for me. I had begun to think about doing medicine, although I hadn't yet finally made up my mind.

Our lessons took place secretly in the loft, and we lived in constant fear of discovery. As well as the academic subjects, we also studied languages. The delightful Mrs Karczewska taught us how to cope with men – in English! "Just be patient, girls," she would tell us. "Remember the struggle *I* had. I had to fight to get my man." She would go on to recount how for thirty years she had been engaged to Mr Karczewski, until she had at last got the absent-minded old scholar to marry her.

Then in 1944, the Germans slipped up again. Wanting to move the 'guinea-pigs' as far away as possible, perhaps so as to be able to dispose of us the more easily when the time came, they moved us to block 32, the very end block at the furthermost corner of the camp. It had the huge advantage of being a corner site, which could be approached only from one direction. This meant that when the SS came to search the block, our look-outs could warn us long before they arrived.

It was in fact a special block, the N N ('Nacht und Nebel') block, for prisoners under sentence of death who were due to disappear from the face of the earth – *in Nacht und Nebel*: under cover of darkness. Apart from ourselves, the block comprised a group of Russian women – actually prisoners of war taken at the Front – and a few French and Norwegians.

The block-leader, Knoll, was a German Communist, who had doubtless once been inspired by idealism. But she had been in prison for eight years, and in that time a great many ideals can go to the wall. Knoll, one of the bloodhound breed, was a terrible thorn in our sides, but luckily for us, she was also a bit stiff in the joints, and we (or at least some of us) were able to out-run her on many occasions.

By now we knew for sure that our list of experimentees and executed had reached its intended destination. Parcels of sugar and dried fruit began coming in from the Red Cross in Geneva, and luxury parcels of sardines from Portugal – specially for the experimentees. Best of all were the Fribourg parcels with their printed announcement that the Holy Father sent us his blessing. The camp went wild – and so did the Germans. We knew now that the boys from the Stalag had been as good as their word, and that our families also would know what to do with the lists we had sent them. In addition Aka Kołodziejczak, an American citizen, had been released from the camp in December 1943, and before leaving had committed names, dates and details to memory.

Convinced, however, that we would never return home, we did something rather bizarre: we drew up a last will and testament. The idea was Władka's. We drew up the will, and – on the assumption that we would not survive and that the Germans would lose the war – added a request that our wishes should be respected in the context of German reparations to Poland. We requested that a school should be founded, a first-class educational establishment

136

for women. Its purpose would be to educate girls in such a way that they would be incapable of fighting wars or of lending themselves to criminal experiments on human beings. The will was signed by all the 'guinea-pigs' and went winging on its way to the world outside . . . Perhaps it is still stowed away safely somewhere . . .

In the spring of 1944, it was beginning to seem more and more probable that Germany would lose the war; and in the camp the battle was on for survival.

A strange atmosphere prevailed in block 32. With its assortment of mixed-race prisoners, all under sentence of death, the place had become a battleground for a Franco-Polish rivalry which expressed itself in a variety of strange ways, and with each nationality determined to flaunt its 'specialness'. This antagonism was probably most apparent when both groups were in the wash-room. On one side stood a row of naked young women – Poles and Russians (with whom we had become very friendly) – washing themselves all over with ice-cold water. And on the other side, fully-dressed French women, painting their faces with beetroot juice – God knows where they got it from! – and washing only their hands. (The term 'French wash' is part of my vocabulary even today!) We did our best to keep our distance from them, and in the end, divided the wash-room into two sections. One end for the Poles and Russians, the other for the French.

International relations in our block were becoming interesting. We struck up a very warm relationship with the Norwegians. They were wonderfully solid, helpful, cultured women, and even the least sophisticated of them showed great sensitivity and tact. The Belgians, forever squabbling with the French, were extremely pleasant and kind. The Dutch – well, the young ones were not so bad, but the older women I found difficult: spiteful and boring. As far as we could, we avoided them. The Czech women didn't actually live with us in the block, so our friendships with them were more casual.

On the whole the 'guinea-pigs' now enjoyed the favour

of the whole camp – a factor which proved to be crucial during the last days of Ravensbrück. But life was still very difficult. No more parcels and letters were coming in, and we had no news at all of our families and friends. We were hungry once again. It's easy now to write the words: 'the days passed . . .' but harder, if you were not there, to appreciate the grinding reality behind those words.

Even optimists were silent now: even Mrs Chrobakowa who had always slept with her shoes on, so as to be ready for the moment of liberation. Even she had stopped talking about the end of the war.

That event, however near it might be, was, as far as we were concerned, lost in the mists of infinity. In fact, the longer it went on, the worse conditions became, for there are limits to human endurance. We knew only that the battle-front was now somewhere near our own homes, and our anxiety about our families was boundless.

Then came the Warsaw Insurrection. The tension of those days was indescribable! Furtively we listened to radio bulletins, and sometimes even managed to purloin a German newspaper. We didn't know what to believe, but it was not long before we were provided with eye-witness accounts of the events. Massive transports of 'evacuees' arrived from Warsaw, pregnant women, children . . . The children came first. Polish children! It was so many years since we had seen a child. The women went crazy . . .

The 'guinea-pigs' were put to guarding the new anti-aircraft ditches which had been dug at the far end of the camp. It was a good job, enabling us to walk freely round the camp, wearing camp-police arm-bands. Within the camp, our position was now fairly strong. We were the only well-organised group, and we had friends everywhere, in all the most important and useful jobs. We were old hands, high in the hierarchy of camp prisoners.

We arranged for one of the external transports to bring us in a camera and a film. One sunny day, we gathered in the utmost secrecy at one end of the camp, and, with hearts thudding against our breasts, took photographs of the legs that had been worst mutilated. We hid the film carefully and smuggled it out to our boys in the Stalag. The camera belonged to Nina, but once we had shot our only film it was of no further use. All the same, we hid it safely with the rest of our illicit property.

In our new role as police-guardians, we did our best to care for the transports coming in from Warsaw, and taught them how to get by in the camp. Sometimes we managed to hide a few of their treasures for them; souvenirs, photographs, wedding-rings and watches. We took buckets full of water out to them, when they had to stand in the blazing heat. And later on, when they had been allocated to their blocks, we made sure to look after them as well as we could.

However, our initial enthusiasm for the Warsaw 'heroines' soon evaporated. I overheard one woman talking about the 'niceness' of the Gestapo; another begged me to hide her favourite photograph which turned out to be a picture of herself taken with a German soldier. I tore up her precious memento, and from then on we looked on the Warsaw transports with a more jaundiced eye, becoming more selective about whom we would help. Little by little, our earlier admiration changed to suspicion. Events had made it difficult for us to love our neighbour with a straightforward, uncomplicated love.

On the whole, though, we did try to save them from work in the armaments factory, for although the food was better there, for us it was the worst work imaginable. We couldn't stop ourselves thinking about the people those bullets were intended for, and the more sensitive souls among us would have preferred to starve to death rather than agree to do such work.

And we *were* starving once more. Life was very hard. The parcels had long ago dried up. There were many more women in the camp, but only the same number of beds as before. We slept five to a bed, then six to two beds in two shifts. Epidemics broke out. Many of the French women died, but surprisingly few Poles. Obviously our insistence on daily cold showers had strengthened our resistance to disease. Typhus, scarlet fever, measles – childhood ills –

thinned out the ranks of women no less successfully than the SS themselves.

Then began the time of the terrible starvation-dysentery, which would torment us right to the very last days. The sewers – built for one tenth the present numbers – were woefully inadequate; and mounds of excrement, foul, stinking bogs, piled up outside the blocks. Filth, famine and, inevitably, fleas plagued us. Lice too. Swarms of them.

The end of the war was so near and yet so far. They began bringing in prisoners evacuated from smaller camps: thin, starving women, all skin and bone, brutalised cattle, who pounced like animals on anything edible. Our relatively clean, quiet block was invaded by a large number of these new arrivals and we had to form a vigilante group around the cauldrons of soup to protect those carrying them from attack. They would fling themselves on the cauldrons of soup, spilling the contents on to the ground as they fought among themselves, then falling on all fours to lick the remains off the dusty street. Even the authorities became aware of what was going on, and provided carts for the cauldrons, and guards to protect their passage.

We were hungry too, and like them we were no more than skin and bone, but no Polish woman ever attacked another for food. Not, at least, until the Auschwitz transports arrived.

Since the arrival of the Warsaw transports, there had been quite a lot of children about, mainly Polish or gypsy, with a few stray Jewish youngsters, all of them under thirteen. In time there were about three hundred and fifty of them, and we resolved at all costs to make their lives a bit easier.

I can't remember now whether it was the Red Cross or some other organisation that had sent some milk for the children, but we 'guinea-pigs' were given the job of distributing it. We were considered to be loudmouthed but honest and unlikely to drink the milk meant for the children.

The trouble we had, both with the milk and the children! On the surface, it was a simple matter of doling out half-litres of milk. Nothing to it! But it turned out to be impossible: swarms of dark, agile kids would hurl themselves at us, and that would be the end of the whole consignment of milk. We tried various ruses. In the end, we locked the children inside the block, and let them out one at a time, giving them their milk in the doorway and making them drink it up then and there.

Even so, we never had enough. We tried giving each one a little less, but it never worked out right and we were still short. I remember once, a little gypsy boy with a veritable moustache of milk all over his mouth, coming up and saying:

"Please, miss, I didn't get any."

"What do you mean, you didn't get any?"

"Well, my brother got some, but I didn't." As if on cue, a second child, exactly like the first, stepped forward. I didn't know which one had had the milk, and which hadn't – or had managed only a taste. The little imps would climb back inside the block through the window and rejoin the queue. They were so alike, there was no way of telling them apart.

By January 1945 there were sure signs that the camp was falling apart. We could sense the war coming to an end, and more and more we were allowing ourselves the luxury of contemplating the prospect of freedom. The more in-curable optimists were blatantly making plans for the future . . . Bogna, however, would entertain no talk about getting out: they would shoot us rather than let us live to tell the tale, she stated categorically. But the rest of us had begun to think it unlikely. After all, they could have shot us ages ago if they'd wanted. So perhaps they didn't intend to, after all . . .

On 15 January, they executed several women from the Warsaw transport. There was stalemate on the fighting front, and every moment's delay might mean the difference between life and death for us. Amongst those shot that day was Halina Wolfart, a beautiful girl with honey-gold eyes and a luminous personality. She had known the day before, and so had we all, though none of us had found the courage to talk to her about it. What does one say to a talented young woman of twenty who knows that tomorrow she is going to be shot? In restless silence we had just stayed with Halina; and she, though pale, was quite calm.

Blind rage almost choked us. Were we to die now, in 1945, when the war was almost over? We felt exceedingly bitter about the death of Halina, who had been such a radiant, charming girl, so full of the joy of living. What a monstrous irony!

Three weeks later, it was our turn. As before, the list had been sent from the Political Department the previous day and all our names were there – all the 'guinea-pigs' and a few other women from our transport. The camp messenger read out the list, ordering the above-named prisoners to stay in the block that day but present themselves at headquarters next morning.

Total, unimaginable silence followed the messenger's departure. I looked at Cesia's face and it was grey. Not pale, but an ashen grey. Just before the list had been read out, Władka had been talking about the mesmerising effect of the prospect of imminent death. Władka was not on the list, but I was there . . . and Krysia too. All of us who'd been operated on were on that list.

"Tomorrow I am going to die," I told myself – and the idea seemed so bizarre and improbable that I laughed aloud. The woman standing next to me looked at me as though I had gone mad.

I decided that I had better prepare myself for death. I went to say goodbye to Mrs Zofia Kahlowa and asked her to pass on my last words . . . I can't recall what they were now, but I remember that she got very upset and burst into tears. She, who had always shown such quiet courage, cried out broken-heartedly:

"No, children, no, it's not possible. You can't die now! There *is* some justice in the world, and that would be utterly unjust."

142

"What about Halina?" I asked quietly.

That silenced her, and with a shaking hand she traced the sign of the cross on our foreheads, Krysia's and mine. She was weeping . . . But we stayed calm.

Lodzia Czajkowska fell on my neck, sobbing loudly. She was a strapping peasant girl to whom we had often given bits of food from our parcels, since she never got any of her own. She was so choked with sobbing that we had to shout to get her to stop. Her name wasn't on the list – she hadn't been operated on.

Lodzia's sobs set everyone else off, and soon everyone was awash. It's not really an exaggeration to say that the whole camp wept. Hard-faced, silent women who had previously shown no sign of emotion, broke down and cried like children.

That night, the women of every block discussed the situation, and sent secret messengers to us. An incredible, unheard-of thing – the whole camp had decided that we were to be saved. Women of all nationalities were determined that the 'guinea-pigs' would not die now, so near to the end.

Where the idea first came from, I don't know. But at all events, the whole camp had decided that we were to disappear that very night. They would take collective responsibility for us, for as long as we remained on the run.

"Run off, all of you, make yourselves scarce," they urged. But running away was not all that easy. The walls were smooth, the tops covered with high-tension wire, and we knew that there was no point in trying to get over them. We should have to hide somewhere inside the camp. The others left it to us, we could hide wherever we had a mind to.

It was no longer just a question of saving our own lives, but of preserving evidence. We were all determined that at least one of us would remain as a living testimony to what had been done.

We discussed the possibilities as night wore on. The Russians in our block gave us their ration of soup for

supper, saying: "You'll need all your strength now, girls."
(By contrast, there were some prisoners who suggested that the block-leader should give them our rations, since we'd obviously be dead by next day.) Szura, an electro-mechanic, promised that the lights would go out at next morning's roll-call.

It was Władka's fault that I cried all night long. She came and begged me at great length to agree to her suggestion: to exchange numbers at next day's roll-call. She was an old woman at the end of her life, she insisted, whereas I was a young one at the beginning of mine; she had not been operated on, whereas I would be needed to bear witness; she even pretended that she had cancer and was going to die soon anyway, that there was no one dependent on her, no one waiting for her to return . . .

I wept and for a long time could not sleep. I had explained to her that it was out of the question, that if I agreed to her suggestion I should never know another moment's peace of mind, that I would not even have the courage to go on living. In the end we decided that both she and I would go to our deaths next day, but that Krysia should remain behind. Krysia must survive to tell the tale; and Władka would take her place.

Krysia would not agree. However, early next morning, we packed her off to Władka's block, explaining that the fewer 'guinea-pigs' left in our block, the easier it would be to hide them.

A couple of hours later we took our place in the line. There was an expression – the faintest glimmer of a smile – in Władka's eyes, which at first I couldn't decipher. Then I suddenly understood: she was wearing Krysia's number – 7708.

It was dark as night that early February morning, and we stood in total silence. The overseer moved from one block to the next, followed by a group of SS men. They're coming near, holding a single sheet of paper in their hands. We know only too well whose names they are going to read out. Silence . . . silence . . . waiting . . . they're getting nearer . . .

I grab Władka's hand . . . the overseer's right by us now . . .

Then suddenly – indescribable hubbub and shouting. The lights go out. We are left in pitch darkness amid the screams of a thousand women. Chaos beyond description, and a din straight out of hell.

Szura had kept her promise.

Day after day, for a whole week, she did the same thing. Though the SS kept careful watch, the lights always went out at roll-call. Always the darkness, and the infernal racket that made it impossible for them to count us or see who was missing.

We had decided on a fight to the death. The Germans made an all-out effort to defeat us, holding extra headcount roll-calls, closing all the camp thoroughfares so as to catch us in their net. The watchword, 'they're after the guinea-pigs' was understood by everybody, and the alarm was raised many times a day. Almost everyone took part in the game, that fearful game of hide-and-seek which we played until the end of April 1945 when we simply had to disappear from the camp.

At first we just took off our numbers and hid – thanks to the magnificent efforts of our Polish block-leaders and others. But I couldn't bear being in hiding. I sat up in the loft for half a day, then decided I'd rather be shot than just sit there, doing nothing. So Krysia and I went out into the camp. We dressed up as Goldstücks – my hair was very long at that time, so I plaited it over my forehead, assumed a blank expression, tied a scarf under my chin, Ukrainian fashion, and went off to visit Władka.

I went up to her in the street, muttering to myself: "Mm, it's good, ever so good, I'll eat every scrap", just as the Goldstücks did. Władka drew away in disgust and dislike. But I came closer. She frowned – then burst out laughing as she recognised me. After that, I felt sure that the policewomen would never penetrate my disguise. And they didn't, even though I roved quite freely all over the camp.

They had recently evacuated Auschwitz and driven the

survivors into our camp, crowding them into an immense shed in the middle of the compound. That Auschwitz transport almost certainly saved our lives: nobody knew how many women were there, so we could safely take refuge in their makeshift hangar.

One Sunday morning they sprang yet another extra roll-call on us. The cries of "They're after the guinea-pigs" had barely died away when the SS and their dogs came on the scene. Silence . . . Krysia, Jadzia and I were standing inside the block, and in front of us sat a row of elderly French women. (Ever since the Red Cross had visited the camp, the older women had been allowed to sit during the interminable roll-calls.)

SS men were everywhere . . . They encircled our block. Nothing to be done – there were six of us in there, the other 'guinea-pigs' having melted into thin air. I leaned over and spoke to Jadzia: "Look, you pick up Germaine and throw her at that chap on the left, and I'll chuck that other old girl at his pal on the right."

Softly, we began to count, one, two, three – and then yelled: "Look out, guinea-pigs." Where I found the strength to throw both the old woman and her chair at the SS man I shall never know. But Jadzia and I both did it at the very same moment; then we all six ran through the sudden gap in the SS ranks like bats out of hell. I've never in all my life run faster. Like greased lightning, we sped into the middle of a crowd of Auschwitz prisoners who had been watching through a crack in their hangar wall. They rose splendidly to the occasion. Never have I undressed and dressed again with such lightning speed. (The Auschwitz women were in civilian clothes.) Someone handed me a red coat, gave me a quick change of hair-do and rapidly inked a tattoo mark on my fore-arm – the number of someone who had died on the long death-march out of Auschwitz camp. I was safe.

It went on like that for days. The fear and tension were exhausting, yet at the same time, they kept us on our toes. We had been starved and tortured; but this new life-and-death struggle made us feel human again. At long last we had taken our lives into our own hands. It was like being reborn.

The others didn't understand at all. Bogna said I was being an idiot, showing off and playing the fool instead of staying hidden. But I couldn't bear to stay in hiding for a single moment. I had to do something, had to give myself the illusion of being in control of my fate. We'd had a bellyful of being pushed around, and now I wanted to taste freedom. I wanted the right to choose. I *needed* to do just what I wanted, for the sole and simple reason that it was what I wanted to do.

At first Władka tried to force me to stay hidden, but after long arguments she eventually gave up. In the end she came to understand that for me it was the only possible way . . . So I continued my roamings.

On one occasion, the shouted warning: "They're hunting guinea-pigs again," came when we were in the new part of the camp, a long way from our own block, and with nowhere to hide. There were some crates standing in a corner. I up-ended one of them over Krysia and slipped under a second one myself . . . Whistles, barking dogs, shouting SS men – and sudden silence. One of the dogs ran right up to my crate and began barking over it. I don't know how long he stood there barking, but in the end I got fed up and could stand it no longer. I wasn't going to sit there and wait for the SS to catch me. Jumping out of the crate, I stamped my foot in fury: "Get out of here!" I yelled.

Those dogs had been specially trained to attack us. I looked round: we were on a street corner, invisible from the front. I couldn't see any SS men. I went up to the dog – a huge Alsatian, which still haunts my dreams – stared it straight in the eye, and said: "If you don't get the hell out, I'll strangle you with my bare hands." I could hardly believe my eyes . . . the animal cowered back, put its tail between its legs and slunk off. That dog had scared the living daylights out of me.

We breathed a sigh of relief. Once again we'd got away with it!

20

They went on looking for us, and never once did they think to look at our legs. Perhaps they were preoccupied with the war, or just plain stupid but I would walk right past the guards' barracks, dressed as a Ukrainian or a gypsy, and no one ever asked us to remove our stockings . . .

At the same time, our two delegates, Bajka and Jadzia, were conducting fruitless diplomatic discussions on our behalf with the commandant. They went and told him that we had no intention of coming forward, because we knew we would be executed if we did so. The commandant was furious at this and shouted that we were nothing but a pack of hysterical women, and that all they wanted to do was to evacuate us in their first transport to Gross Rosen camp. It was true that some groups were already being evacuated from Ravensbrück, and we had managed to slip one or two of the ambulant 'guinea-pigs' into some of these transports. However, to get the better of the commandant, our friends replied that Gross Rosen was already liberated; that in any case we would rather stay with our friends in the camp; and that we were not looking for privileged treatment of any kind. And that was flat!

Then one day, the SS surrounded sixteen of us and drove us into a corner with our backs to the wall. "This is it," I thought. "This time, there is absolutely nothing we can do." There was no possibility of saving ourselves . . . In my pocket I had a tiny bag of Polish soil. I held on to it hard. "Sentimental idiot," I chided myself.

The Russian women were in front, ready to defend us if it came to a struggle. We stood immediately behind them. Those in the back row were trying to force a gap in the wire mesh that separated the camp from the rewir; and two of them actually managed to slip into the rewir through the gap they had made.

But a moment later, the camp police came and stood in that spot. Nothing could now save us . . .

We stood still, waiting, as we had so often waited, for certain death.

Suddenly – how can I possibly describe what happened next? Suddenly, from the direction of the camp's main street, came a screaming mob of embattled women who hurled themselves at the SS cordon. They went through that cordon like a knife through butter; and without a second's hesitation, we clambered through the gap in the wire, and into the sheltering embrace of the Auschwitz shed. Afterwards we learned what had happened: block-leader Bortnowska had announced to her starving flock that over in that corner the SS men were handing out bread. The hungry women had simply headed off in search of something to eat. They knew nothing at all about the 'guinea-pigs'' plight, but their action had certainly saved our lives.

That night we didn't return to the block, but stayed with our saviours in the hangar. The SS went on looking for us, but found no trace of us anywhere in the camp.

And it was thanks to the unprecedented solidarity of the camp; to the co-operation of all the women, Poles and non-Poles alike; and especially to the efforts of our own block officials and of Mother Liberakowa, that all the 'guinea-pigs' soon had guaranteed, regular hiding-places. The camp was whole-hearted in its protection of the 'guinea-pigs'. Everyone helped in some way, some deliberately, others by default. From the moment when the heroic decision was taken to protect us, there had been a dramatic – and universal – change of mood. Gone were the lifeless zombies; in their place were women with flushed, animated faces, whispering excitedly and with a tense wariness about the eyes. Full of fight and spirit, we were human beings again.

Some of the 'guinea-pigs' spent their nights in the clothes depot, lying on shelves and covered with dresses and underwear. They lay there shivering with cold in the freezing February temperatures. Others lay on third-tier bunks in the loft over the official servants' quarters.

There was another hiding-place, too – in the transport block where the new arrivals were housed. The Polish block-leader hid us among these latest comers, the Yugoslavs and Ukrainians who understood no language but their own. One day all the women, including a handful of 'guinea-pigs', were turfed out of this block and a selection was made for the newly-built gas-chambers. This was only the first of many between then and Easter and the women were made to stand in rows while the selection was made. All the elderly, the sick and the maimed were sent off to be gassed.

Jadzia, one of the 'guinea-pigs' who had been hiding in the transport block, had an enormous scar along her shin; and her leg was now badly deformed as a consequence. With barbed wire surrounding the transport block, escape was clearly impossible. No one had been expecting selections to be made from among the new arrivals, and we had no hope at all that Jadzia's useless leg would escape attention.

Mrs Halina Chorążyna and Stenia stood next to her, trying to conceal her legs. On the other side of the wire stood Śledź, nosey as always, but this time ashen-faced as never before. The doctor was coming nearer. I shall never know how Oberheuser came to miss seeing Jadzia's legs, but miss them she did. And when she had gone by without dragging Jadzia from the ranks, the poor girl, usually as tough as nails, burst into tears, her whole body shuddering with relief.

Finally, they called another head-count roll-call, in a last-ditch attempt to round up the elusive 'guinea-pigs'. We made careful preparations. Those of us with the worst-damaged legs – Stenia, Bogna, Wojtka, Jadzia, Dzido, Piasecka and Marczewska – took a spade and dug themselves in underneath the block, armed with stolen blankets and a little food. Brr . . . It was cold and smelled foul – the plumbing had long ago given up on the overcrowded camp, and women simply relieved themselves right there at the side of the block. Huge, black rats with bare, slimy tails were scuttering about. There was the thud of earth being shovelled over the girls, when suddenly Wojtka, a brave, stalwart lass, shouted "Stop!" in a loud, hysterical voice and burst into tears as she grabbed the spade from Stenia's hands. After a while, she calmed down and explained apologetically: "I'm sorry, but I just felt I was being buried alive." I couldn't bring myself to tell her that it had seemed like that to me too.

For seven days and seven nights they stayed buried in that cold, dank hole. Dzidzia was attacked by violent cramps, but dared not so much as move her head.

On the seventh day, one of them came to me and said she could stand it no longer. (Krysia, Jadzia Kamińska and I took turns as messengers for the 'guinea-pigs'.) "Tomorrow," she announced, "I will go to the office and give myself up to be shot. I can't take any more." And she was sick where she stood.

That same day, Dziuba came running from the office with news: "Girls, girls, there's going to be a hell of a lot of changes round here." The buried-alive 'guinea-pigs' crawled out of their hole . . .

And things certainly did begin to happen.

The commandant summoned ten of the experimentees (in alphabetical order), ostensibly in order to set them free. We ignored his invitation, thanking him (via the camp messenger) for his concern, but insisting that we'd rather stay in the camp with everyone else right to the end. We preferred to stay in the camp, we told him, because life was so enjoyable there!

Then he tried a different tack, summoning Marysia Broel-Plater by name and handing her a piece of paper on which was written:

I, the under-signed, hereby declare that the scar on my leg was caused by an accident at work.

If she signed, she was told, she would be immediately set free. Marysia refused. She knew the 'guinea-pigs' were right behind her, and in any case she didn't for one moment trust the commandant

Then he tried sending for our delegates, Bajka and Jadzia. When they walked into the commandant's office, they saw a stranger in civilian clothes, with a briefcase full of documents. The commandant whispered something to him and, indicating the women's legs, said that these two weren't all that bad; the others were in far worse shape. The strange man did not say a word.

Jadzia, whose courage often bordered on the reckless, then spoke out. She said that the whole world knew about those experiments, and reminded the commandant about the parcels that had come from Geneva, from Sweden and from Portugal solely for the victims of the experiments. She reminded him of the blessing sent by the Pope. And she dared finally to say that the war was as good as over, and that if they were to shoot us now, the consequences for themselves would be catastrophic. Then playing her trump card, she suggested that there just might be extenuating circumstances in the commandant's case, if he made it his business now to make sure that the 'guinea-pigs' stayed alive.

He interrupted her, saying it was not for him to decide, he had his orders from Berlin, but that perhaps they could reach some sort of understanding . . . Then he dismissed them both.

A day or so later the commandant personally came up to Bajka in the street (she and Jadzia were not in hiding, as they wanted to be permanently available to speak for us) and told her that Berlin had more important things on their minds just now than the plight of 'guinea-pigs'. We could well believe it. Considering that the whole Third Reich was falling about their ears, Berlin must have had better things to think about than the fate of a few score Polish women experimented on in Ravensbrück camp. So, all we could do was wait, said the commandant, and he gave us his word of honour that nothing would happen to us meanwhile.

For once we believed him, and the 'guinea-pigs' slowly

began to emerge from their holes. But we were fifteen short – the ones we had slipped into the out-going transports – and once again our numbers at roll-call wouldn't tally, so Joanna and Jadzia took charge of 'borrowing' bodies from other blocks to make up our numbers. All the decent blocks took part in this operation. Mrs Siasia Schöneman started a 'Save the Corpses' movement. She simply hid the bodies of those who had died, while reporting that they had been sent to the crematorium; and we propped them up during roll-call. It was the final service that the dead could render to the living.

Sometimes we were even helped out by the rewir workers, who were exempt from roll-calls.

In other blocks the numbers might not always tally; but in ours they always did. At worst we were nine instead of ten. Broad-shouldered Russian girls would cheerfully fill any gaps. They did not hesitate to risk their lives on our behalf.

Yet it was not until the French *Nacht und Nebel* transport left the camp that we finally got our numbers sorted out. At the last moment we managed to add the names of several extra French women to the already-checked numbers on their list. Then at last our numbers tallied. But that was not until the beginning of April, by which time, the whole camp's fight to save the lives of the 'guinea-pigs' was close to being won.

But the 'guinea-pigs' were to be involved in one last revolt, this time over food parcels. Canada had sent six thousand parcels for the French, the Polish Jews and the Poles. The French women and the Jews got theirs. Then Binz sent for the 'guinea-pigs', saying that the Polish parcels would be given out next day, but that we could have ours separately now so as to avoid being trampled in the crush. She did indeed give us our parcels, and the more impatient ones among us started in on them that same evening.

But next morning, when the Polish women were given only one parcel between two, the 'guinea-pigs' were up in arms. We immediately re-packed our own parcels, loaded them on to a cart and took them to the main office. (All this, though we were unspeakably hungry. There had been no food parcels for seven long months.) We announced that we would not accept the parcels unless every Polish woman was given a whole one for herself.

The commandant was angry. That's what he got for making sure that the 'guinea-pigs' got their parcels, he complained. Our spokeswomen said that it was kind of him to think of us, but the parcels had been intended for all the Polish women; they had seen the list the day before.

We returned proudly along the street, and were greeted with enthusiasm all the way. People were shouting in different languages and wanting to shake us by the hand. Fifteen hundred of the six thousand parcels were given out. The SS men took the rest. That was the last 'guinea-pig' rebellion, and it has remained the one that our fellow-prisoners remember best. Someone cried, "Long live the 'guinea-pigs'!" Starving women were grateful for the stand we had taken, and found enough strength to escort us in procession, cheering as they went. We had touched their hearts.

Throughout this intervening drama we hadn't entirely accepted the commandant's word, we continued to smuggle 'guinea-pigs' secretly out of the camp. Then at last, it was our turn and Władka strongly recommended us to leave with a transport of Auschwitz women: we already had the numbers of people who'd died inked on to our fore-arms (there was no tattooing done in Ravensbrück). But I didn't want to go. I wanted to stay behind with Władka and see the whole thing through to the end.

Władka, however, overcame my resistance with one simple argument: "Get Krysia away from here." So we went.

Our troubles began right at the start. Even by the second day, it was obvious that our numbers were no good – their owners were still alive. Suddenly, from a few rows in front

154

of me, I heard someone give my own false name and number. In fear and trembling I waited my turn. Whatever could I say? I shouted the first number that came into my head. – Nobody checked it. – And the first name I could think of: Danuta Szarecka. Luckily, there were no Auschwitz lists and the Germans were still making out a new one.

That night they herded us into a large barn where they kept us for several days with no food, no water, no sanitary arrangements of any kind. It was dreadful. Krysia spent the first night weeping softly against my knees. There was no room to lie down, we could only sit. Then they took us to Neustadt-Glewe, a small camp purpose-built next to a factory, and locked us into an empty room.

We found our new conditions very difficult to get used to. The Auschwitz women fought over their food. In Ravensbrück, the so-called 'luxury' camp, where the 'guinea-pigs' had kept their self-respect, and had cared more for books and learning than for soup, fighting over food had been unheard-of. We didn't even know how to set about it. So we got nothing to eat. Had it not been for Polina, a Russian doctor from Ravensbrück who was working in the camp as a pathologist performing autopsies, we would never have survived.

At first I was able to buy bread for Krysia from the SS. It was very dear: one small piece from a loaf cost twenty gold dollars. But we had found some gold coins in Ravensbrück and I had managed to prevent their being discovered, despite frequent strip-searches, by sticking them to the soles of my feet. During wash-time and throughout the searches, no one thought of looking there, even though the guards' search techniques were terrifyingly brutal.

Having also got those dollars past all the control points at the gates, I had used them to buy bread for Krysia from an SS man. But now I had no more dollars and no more bread.

The problem of hunger in Neustadt-Glewe was infinitely worse than it had been in Ravensbrück. It was only a small camp, cut off from a supply base, and rations were severely limited. We had nothing but soup made from potato peelings and a slice of bread each day. Krysia and I were even worse off than anyone else, because we never got any of the soup. I can't remember how long we stayed there, but each day brought us closer to the stark reality of starving to death. If the war hadn't ended when it did, the end would have been too late for us.

The nights were noisy and stifling; space was so restricted that we could not lie down but had to sit hunched-up. It was only thanks to the kindness of Mrs Neli J. who let us lean back against her legs that we got any sleep at all, however fitful. There were no beds, and in any case there was no possibility of getting undressed. A bare floor and a vast number of half-dead people jamming it solid. Once again the lice began to increase and multiply.

One day I collapsed from weakness. Someone, maybe Krysia, took me to the rewir.

The rewir . . . It was exactly like the one in Ravensbrück. Everyone knew that people came here to die. And I was put where the dying waited for death. I was suffering from the dreadful starvation-dysentery and could eat nothing. Absolutely nothing. Even though Polina once brought me some soup, and on another occasion a piece of charcoal bread, I simply could not eat. Then in the end, no one even looked in on us, and no food was brought in since none of us near-corpses was capable of swallowing.

I had been put on a bunk bed. Above, below and together with me were women who, like myself, were dying of starvation. In the same bed as myself was a French woman, or maybe she was a gypsy, I can't be sure. A small, dark woman, a young girl really, not much more than a child.

During the night, one of the women in the bunk above me suddenly fell crashing to the ground. I thought she had fallen out of bed until I realised that the woman in bed with her had thrown out her corpse.

Next day, my own little bed-fellow began to die – the little gypsy whose name I didn't even know. She was ice-cold, and my first thought was to throw her body out of the bed. Then an immense pity for her seized me. I covered her with our one and only blanket, and she lay beside me till she died. I don't remember how many days and nights we lay there. By the next day I couldn't have managed to throw her corpse out of the bed, even if I'd wanted to. I was too weak.

One after another they died, until at last it seemed that there was nobody left alive. No one looked in on us, except Krysia pressing her pale face against the window. Or did I only imagine that she was there? I would make a superhuman effort to wave my hand in her direction. But eventually I was unable even to do that.

Yet I didn't die. And in some strange way, the more conscious of my physical weakness I became, the clearer I was able to think. Of course my thoughts were mainly about death. As I lay there waiting to die, I pursued all those lines of thought which had so often been cut off in mid-stream in the camp. Never before nor since, have my thoughts been as clear and lucid. Though, of course, I may simply have been delirious.

One day, a man came and cut through the camp's barbed wire with shears.* "Girls, you're all free!" he shouted. "You idiot," said a companion. "What are you shouting for? This place is a morgue."

Yet I was alive and conscious. Lying there, with the gypsy girl's icy corpse for company, I had finally decided to study medicine. It sounds crazy. At a time when I was only hours away from dying of starvation, here I was planning my future life. It's the way I am: the thought of death arouses in me the will not only to live but to live life more intensely.

It was a long time before I could grasp the fact that the war was over, that we were free . . . The reality of those men cutting through the wire had not impinged on me at all. I had wondered dully what it was all about and what it could possibly have to do with me.

* Neustadt-Glewe camp was liberated by the Russians on 8 May 1945. The Americans were only three miles away at the time.

I got to my feet, swaying unsteadily, when Krysia came in. The sun was shining . . .

In front of the barracks was an extraordinary sight: a mob of screaming women breaking into the stores and hurling themselves on to the food. Some of the weaker ones were being crushed underfoot. We stood to one side . . . They were snatching food from each other's grasp, pulling each other's hair, tearing each other's flesh with their nails. Blood flowed freely. Would those women survive, I wondered idly, or would they too die within reach of freedom?

Freedom. Somehow the word had no meaning for me just then . . . On the other hand, suddenly I was terribly, irresistibly hungry!

21

While I was still lying at death's door in the rewir, I had often had a rather ridiculous dream – of white semolina in milk; a whole plateful. But I was unable to eat it because it was behind a thick pane of glass. Suddenly I felt a craving for semolina. "Krysia," I said, "I want some semolina." There was something in my tone of voice and the expression on my face that brooked no argument. "Right, let's go and look for some," she replied. We looked. At first we searched through the overseers' and SS barracks, but others – a mob of hungry women, in fact – had got there before us and turned the place over. Scarcely able to put one foot in front of the other, we almost crawled to a small town which had not yet been cleared out, though its shops and stores had been broken into and partially ransacked. Those shops were full of food, tins of meat and preserves, but I wasn't interested. All I craved was semolina, and I craved it with a fanatical and incomprehensible stubbornness (which I now recognise as an inspired instinct that certainly saved our lives!).

Exhausted, we sat down on some steps and watched a straggling column of Germans lay down their arms . . . Two Russian soldiers and one American to disarm a whole division! The discarded weapons piled up in a growing heap by the bridge, but we were indifferent to the sight. I say 'we', though I can't claim to speak for Krysia. I only know that I myself could not have cared less. I had a raging desire for a plateful of white semolina, and was near to tears because we hadn't found any.

It was growing dark when, at last, in a little shop that had already been vandalised, I found a handful of semolina in an overturned drawer. We tied it up in a handkerchief and set off to walk the four kilometres back to the camp.

I cannot explain why we returned there. Perhaps it was because we had no idea of what else to do.

The camp compound had already been abandoned: only a few women wandered aimlessly around. We made our way to the SS camp and decided to spend the night there. I cooked the semolina in water, without either sugar or salt, and poured it on to plates for Krysia and myself. We began to eat it . . . It may seem hard to believe, but it took us all that evening and all the next day to get through that small amount. I lay on an SS woman's bed, wanting to weep because I now had the semolina and could not bring myself to eat it. Krysia ate nearly a plateful and then fell asleep. I just lay there.

How strange it was, that first night of our freedom; 7 May 1945. Sporadic fighting was still going on, and we could hear the guns. Crowds of ex-prisoners, men and women, came into the camp for the night. They sang, smashed up the camp, lit bonfires and spit-roasted whole sheep and calves. I wondered how they'd come by the sheep, and where so many men had appeared from. I don't know what language they were speaking in, for I just stayed by the window observing everything as though watching a movie.

The men and women finished their feasting. I looked on with interest, but also with incomprehension. Women, among whom I now recognised a few acquaintances, their thin cheeks strangely flushed, began gyrating frantically and tearing the clothes off their horribly emaciated bodies; while the men, no less thin and emaciated, flung themselves upon them. Towards morning they fell asleep still entwined in each other's embrace. "Corpses," I thought suddenly, "they're corpses, they have died there . . .'

I was more right than I knew. By the still-smouldering embers of their bonfire, the bodies lay, their faces contorted with pain. Many of those who had partaken of the feast died of it. Others, rushed off next day by the Red Cross to a nearby hospital, were ill for a very long time, their intestines twisted into hard knots. Thank God I had wanted only to eat semolina.

We spent the next day bent over our semolina – and at last managed to get a whole plateful down.

After three platefuls, our will to live returned, and we set off to explore our surroundings. The Neustadt-Glewe camp was a small labour camp situated near an airfield. On the airfield, camouflaged by trees, stood a few hangars with planes inside. I climbed into one of them and felt a sudden desperate desire to take off. But there was no one to fly us out of that place. Through the trees we spotted a high tower which had been used for parachute practice. We went towards it and began to climb it very slowly. It took us ages to reach the little platform at the top, and when we got there, we were panting and out of breath. I just stood there, stock still.

Before me unfolded an incredible panorama: rolling seas of forest stretching into infinity – and the distant shimmer of a lake. Above the lake stood a little white castle, then more of those green, green woods. How often had I dreamed of forests like that! I filled my lungs with that wonderfully bracing air, and was amazed to hear my own voice shouting: "Free! Free! We're actually free!" The echo came back to us: "Free! Free! Free!" There could be no doubting it now.

All tiredness gone, we ran down the steps. No longer were we grey and haggard skeletons. Colour had returned to Krysia's pale cheeks. With feverish haste we packed our few possessions into bundles and decided to set off for home. At once, immediately, home. To our mothers.

Five of our friends decided to come with us.

Before leaving, we thought we had better have something to eat and find some provisions to take with us. But all we could find was a little bag of dried peas in the loft. Assuming the tones of a leader I announced that I would go and forage for food. Taking a large kitchen knife with me, I set off for the forest.

I ran along the path, confident that I would spot some animal to bag for our dinner. But there were no animals about. At last, in a small water-meadow, I came on the carcass of a horse that had only recently been killed and was still bleeding. It wasn't a fully-grown horse, just a foal, lying there with its neck outstretched, a really pitiable sight. I took a deep breath and went up to it, wondering which part of the carcass I should hack a piece from, and which part would provide the tastiest meat. I made my decision and inserted the knife.

What happened next was so sudden and unexpected that I'm not sure I can describe it. I had been absolutely convinced that I was alone in the forest, and certainly I hadn't seen anyone up till then. But, at the precise moment when I plunged that knife in the carcass, the foal reared up and neighed . . . and a mob of women materialised from nowhere and surrounded us. They fell on my poor foal, silencing it once and for all, tearing it to pieces with their bare hands. I stood to one side, watching them, the knife still in my hand. Ignoring both me and my knife, they tore at the foal with nails and teeth, ripping gobbets of meat away from the skin. Then suddenly everything went quiet again. Nothing remained of the horse but bones. If it hadn't been for those bones, I'd have thought I'd been dreaming.

But I still hadn't found any food . . . I wandered along the edge of the forest and there, in an abandoned house, found some eggs and a few baked potatoes still in the oven. I took them, baking dish and all, and returned to the camp.

The eggs were delicious beyond description: Can you imagine just how good an egg can taste when you haven't seen one for four years?

We then set off with our little bundles, and as we entered a small nearby town, peace was being proclaimed over the loudspeakers. A sentry stopped us. Our moment of choice had arrived. Here we were in no-man's-land, with the Americans on one side, the Russians on the other. They asked us where we wanted to go, and at first I didn't understand the question. What did they mean, where? An officer explained politely that we were free to go wherever we wished, but as far as Krysia and I were concerned, the answer was simple: we wanted to go home.

Some of the women with us hesitated. A few, with no hesitation at all, made off towards the Americans.

And so began our odyssey. They gave us documents stating that we were returning from a concentration camp, and requiring local authorities to give us all possible assistance. Then papers had to be made out for a group leader. Our friends decided that I should be officially confirmed in the role.

With these documents we pressed on. It was 8 May 1945 and who would have guessed that our journey would take another twenty days?

22

May . . . that wonderful first May of freedom! The earth over which we travelled was so beautiful! Flowering orchards, woods sweeping down towards lake shores that suddenly sprang out of nowhere, the scent of sweet-smelling magnolia. That first day was like a dream, a fantasia in sunlight and green.

The white highway, smooth as glass, gleaming in the sun . . .

A little town. Shuttered windows. The Germans keeping indoors, soldiers everywhere on the streets. We ask for the administrative centre and are taken there. I show my group-leader credentials and explain that we have all been experimented on in Ravensbrück, that we can't walk easily because of the pain in our legs, and could they please provide us with horses and carts.

The Russian duty officer was summoned. I looked at him, and went weak at the knees. Gosh, he was a good-looking man!

"Grisha, get some carts for the Ravensbrück girls!"

Grisha flashed me a smile – he had lips like raspberries, big, strong, white teeth, eyes as blue as the sky, and jet-black hair.

"Right, then. Come on."

I followed him . . . through the hallway, into the garden. I imagined we were going to the stables to find some horses, but I was wrong. A long path wound through the orchard, disappearing at length into undergrowth and – a lake glinting in the sun. On the lake, a boat moored by a chain, and on the shore, a little bench covered with leaves and overhung with magnolia. Over there, on the far side of the lake, I saw white rocks and a little castle perched on top.

"It's like a fairy-tale," said Grisha.

I laughed.

He came close. He didn't throw himself on me, or even touch me, just looked with those enormous blue eyes. He was very young, probably even younger than I was. He leaned towards me gently as if to embrace me.

"Kiss me."

"No."

He didn't understand. He looked at me uncomprehendingly from under those long, dark lashes, and said again:

"Kiss me."

"No."

He got angry.

"Why ever not?"

"Because I won't."

"Am I repulsive? Have I got leprosy or something?"

I smiled at him and told him quite truthfully:

"Grisha, you're quite the best-looking man I've ever seen."

"So why won't you kiss me, then?"

"Because I don't want to."

He crumpled his cap in his hand and hurled it into the lake. His face was red. He grabbed hold of my hand, squeezing it hard, hurting me. I cried out with pain, but he paid no attention. Again he asked:

"Why not?"

I looked round. We were quite alone. It was such a beautiful day, the orchard was in bloom . . . What possible explanation could I give him?

"Well, you see, I don't love you."

That calmed him a little. He dropped my hand and asked:

"Why not? I love you very much . . ."

At that moment, he was so terribly attractive, and he spoke the Polish endearment so beautifully.

I tried to explain that I couldn't just fall in love instantly, but he didn't understand.

"Why not? I can."

"Grisha, there's someone else . . ."

At last he got the point and swept out of sight, while I

retrieved his crumpled cap and walked slowly back to the main office where I explained that we would find our own transport.

Off we went. I had decided to look for a horse as my companions weren't able to walk far, and made for the village where I entered the first farmhouse I saw. It was clean and well-kept, not at all like the ones I remembered at home. With sudden nostalgia I thought of the wretched farm-cottages of Podhaly.

There was a horse in the stable but it was lame, with one of its legs bandaged. When I went outside again, a soldier was standing in the farmyard. A cheerful blond chap, stocky and with a lively face.

"Hey, girl, what do you want? A horse?" he asked with a laugh.

"Come on, I'll give you an iron one."

He dragged me, resisting, into a barn.

"Don't be frightened. I'm not going to hurt you."

But I *was* frightened.

There was a bicycle leaning against one of the walls of the barn. A bicycle – that was just what we needed. If only I could get hold of five bicycles! But even this one would be something, we could at least strap our bundles on to it.

"Give it me!" I said, pointing to the bike.

He handed it over, but when I tried to leave he blocked my way.

"Come here, let's make love."

"I don't want to make love."

At first he was cheerful about it, but gradually he became more insistent and his voice lost its jokiness.

"I'll give you a watch."

"I don't want one."

"And a dress . . . and rings! Look!"

Then the recurring refrain:

"Why won't you?"

"Because I don't love you," I said for the second time that day.

He laughed. "Well, you'd better start falling in love with

me right now. I love you. I loved you desperately from the first moment I saw you."

"How desperately?"

"To the death."

It was my turn to laugh, and my laughter clearly riled him.

"Don't you believe in love?"

"Oh yes, I believe in it, but what reason do I have to love you?"

He put his arms round me; but I wriggled away.

"You know, Polish women believe in real love."

"So do I."

"What do you mean, so do you? You want me to pay for the bicycle with love."

"No. I gave you the bicycle for nothing."

"Did you indeed? Well, give it me, then."

I took the bicycle, but again he blocked my path.

"Come on, over there." He pointed to a corner where there was a pile of sweet-smelling hay.

It was my turn to get angry.

"I don't want your bicycle, let me go."

But he wouldn't.

"I love you."

"How much?"

"More than my life."

I laughed again:

"I don't want your life, but I *would* like the bicycle. Don't be mean. A man in love can surely give a woman a bicycle."

"Me? Mean?" he asked indignantly. "Nobody in my family is mean."

"Well then, give me the bicycle!"

At last! He let me have it. We went outside together and I watched him as I got on the bicycle. His face was sad. At least give me a smile, he said.

I smiled at him, and rode the bicycle back to the office. They asked me where I'd got it.

"It was a present."

"A present?"

Incredulous smiles all round, and the question:

"What did you have to give for it?"

"Just a smile."

It didn't worry me that they didn't believe me. I felt happy, and for some reason I was no longer afraid.

We didn't get far that day, and when we stopped for the night, the officers came in pursuit of us. Grisha came first, on his own. We were to get ready, he said; they were coming to have supper with us.

I prepared a corner room on the ground floor, with easy access to a window if we needed to escape, and locked the younger girls in an upstairs attic while Halina and I decided to have supper with the men. Towards nightfall, a slim, dark, Ukrainian girl joined us and sat on a bench against the interior wall. Under the window, the lilac was in bloom, and nightingales sang. It was a lovely night.

A soldier accosted Wiera, our Ukrainian friend, and chased her into the bushes. Minutes later she came out weeping.

I was on edge. The soldier laughed.

Just then, our officer-friend and a few others arrived. Wiera was still sobbing inconsolably. They came up to me and asked:

"Where are the girls?"

"They were frightened and ran away. They're not here."

"Why were they frightened?"

"Why?" I was furious at the question, and answered:

"Because you're all such swine. That girl over there is weeping because one of your men has just raped her."

"What?" The officer blinked. "Which one?"

Without thinking, I pointed to the offender.

"Him."

The officer went up to the man and said something to him. Then he came back to me.

"With us, one pays for that with one's life!"

The nightingale was still singing, but my hands were cold as ice.

They had brought everything with them for supper. Enough vodka to float a ship, wine, and mountains of food. Black caviar. The oldest of the officers sat next to me. Grisha sat opposite, but he ignored me, concentrating on Halina.

There was no electric light, so we had our feast by candlelight. I took one look at those candles and decided not to have anything to drink. I poured it all under the table.

The men got rowdier and more boisterous. My neighbour's name, he told me, was Ivan. At midnight, he proposed. No kidding! He got to his feet, made a speech and . . . asked for my hand in marriage. I thanked him with as much warmth as I could muster, and said that first I would have to go back and see my mother in Warsaw. Fine, he said, we'll go to Warsaw together. I looked at the candle on the table and calculated how many centimetres were left.

There were two beds in the room, white and inviting. Ivan stood up and pointed to one of them, bellowing:

"Ah, here is our nuptial bed, my little Wanda!"

I told him I wouldn't go to bed with him without a marriage-licence.

"You want a priest?"

"Yes! I can't sleep with you till we're married."

By then he was so drunk that he was capable of anything. I whispered to Halina:

"Get close to the window. When the candles go out, we'll make a dash for it."

The candles died with a faint sputter. I hurtled through the window, with the maudlin babbling still going on behind me:

"Wanda, my pet, my darling."

We ran up to the attic, bolted the door, and slept till morning.

When morning came, we decided to snatch a quick breakfast and be off. But before we'd eaten so much as a mouthful, a wagonette drawn by four magnificent horses drove up to the porch, and inside – Oh God, I thought I'd die – inside was my admirer of the night before, wearing white gloves and with an enormous bunch of lilac in his hand. Beside him was a terrified Orthodox priest; the genuine article with a long beard.

I didn't wait to see what would happen. We left by the back door and escaped into the forest.

We walked for miles, pushing our belongings on the bicycle. Our legs hurt and we were very hungry. But there were masses of other hungry refugees like ourselves, and they always seemed to get everywhere before us, eating up all the food like a swarm of locusts.

One day as we trudged wearily along the high road, a convoy of lorries drove by. The last one stopped.

"Where do you want to go, girls?"

"To Poland."

"Get in!"

We got in, together with our precious bicycle that I had won with a smile. We drove along, singing cheerfully at the tops of our voices in the company of seven young soldiers and two older ones. All of a sudden, the truck turned into a side road leading into a wood. It was getting dark and the trees kept out what sun there was. A sudden foreboding made me turn to the officer and ask what we were doing turning into a wood.

"Into the wood? Well, for firewood, of course."

But the other trucks had not gone that way. This one drove deep into the forest and came to a sudden halt.

The men who had till then been chatting to us about the war, stopped talking. The driver got down and called to us:

"Trip's over! Get out!"

They threw our bundles out and drove off. We couldn't understand . . . – until suddenly we heard the truck's engine stop. It had halted somewhere nearby but out of sight. I grabbed Krysia's hand, as it belatedly dawned on us why they had left us in this spot. We huddled together in alarm. The wood just here led into a little copse of young trees. Behind us was dense forest. Ahead, on the far side of the copse, were fields, and far away in the distance we

170

could see the red roofs of houses. Too far away for anyone to be able to hear us.

The men were approaching silently . . . grimly. We huddled even closer and held each other tightly.

"Come on!"

"No fear!"

"Come on!"

"No, we won't!"

I told the girls: "Hold on as tight as you can. If we stick together, they can't rape us."

The oldest of the men had a cigarette in his mouth. I turned to him and spoke pleadingly:

"Perhaps you have a wife and daughter of your own, sir . . ."

He said nothing.

I tried a fresh approach:

"You're a swine. No real soldier would even shake hands with you."

"What? Me?" He lunged closer.

"If your commanding officer were here, he'd shoot you like a dog."

"I haven't even touched you."

It was true, he hadn't – yet!

But he began to close in. Pale, watery eyes, gums bared in a grimace . . . the sight of him scared me to death. In a panic I began bawling him out, calling him every name I could think of. But he didn't react at all . . .

I stopped shouting. A second man was coming up behind him.

"Are you bloody well coming, or aren't you?" he bellowed.

High above us the sun shone and I could hear a lark singing. Everywhere was green. Was it for this that I had spent four long years in a concentration camp, I wondered in despair. Could this be really happening? Oh, God!

"Come here, you filthy hag."

I jerked my head back and the movement sent my hair tumbling in waves down my back. I looked up at the sky. And then I answered him, so calmly that I surprised myself:

"You can shoot me if you want. Perhaps someone somewhere will shoot your sister for the very same reason! But I'll *never* go with you."

I don't know who started it, or if indeed anyone did, for we all seemed to act at precisely the same moment. Suddenly, spontaneously, without even exchanging glances, we all began to scream, in unison, as if we were on the same spring, and so loud that it seemed as if the whole world would hear us. A single scream of – Mama!

A scream so piercing that the men, who had us surrounded now, sprang back . . .

Silence . . . a whole eternity of silence . . . The snap of branches . . . the roar of an engine . . . then silence again, broken only by the song of the lark.

We stood there for some time, not daring to move, and when at last we opened our eyes, there was nobody there. The truck had gone. We were alone. We stood there a moment longer, then walked through the copse to where the fields began. The earth smelled sweet. I threw myself down on the grass and, to my surprise, promptly burst into tears.

After that we never accepted lifts, and travelled always on foot. We didn't even dare go near the villages.

Our legs hurt dreadfully and I had huge blisters on my feet. Those big, clumsy camp boots were not meant for a journey like this one.

We longed to be back at home, yet home seemed so far away . . .

Once we stopped for the night in a little cottage with a garden all around it. We settled down to sleep upstairs, or rather the others did, while I kept watch. (We all took turns to do guard duty.) Two of the girls were lying on a large sofa, with Kawka lying across the end. Zosia Modraczek and I had to sit up. Around midnight, two drunken soldiers pushed their way into the room.

"OK, girls, we're going to sleep here with you."

I checked to make sure that there were only two of them. There was nobody else.

One of them fell on the sofa in a befuddled stupor – right

172

next to Kawka. The other sat beside me, and we talked well into the morning. He even knew the poetry of Mickiewicz, and recited several verses from memory.

Towards morning, Kawka woke up. Only then did she see the inert figure of the soldier lying half-dressed by her side. Her eyes widened in terror.

Then the soldier, roused by her movements, sat up too. In embarrassed confusion, he began to do up his buttons, then he stood up, fumbled in his pockets and produced a handful of coins. Blushing furiously, he pressed them into stunned Kawka's hand and dashed out of the door without a backward glance. His companion, meanwhile, was fast asleep on the table, still exhausted after his sleepless night.

We creased up at the expression on Kawka's face, and we counted up the coins. We'd no idea of what it was worth, but were quite convinced that it amounted to a fortune and we teased Kawka unmercifully about earning so much money with so little effort. Poor thing!

She was never quite sure what had *really* happened that night, and we were enjoying ourselves too much to enlighten her!

23

Hands . . . men's hands, reaching out for me . . . lustful glances . . . oily smiles.

There were so many variations on the theme, so many seemingly innocent approaches to defenceless women.

We had very quickly learned to distinguish between the men who were harmless and those who represented a threat. We could tell from their faces, their gestures, from all sorts of give-aways, I came to know instinctively when to run or get Krysia away, and when it was safe to stay put. I was a barometer, and in time the others got the hang of it too.

When we first came out of the camp, we had a horror of women and an exaggerated idealism about men, because it was so long since we had seen any. But we learned quickly enough.

One night we stopped by the shore of a lake. Very quietly, so as not to be discovered, we dossed down in a canoe-hire boat-house. But next morning someone found us. A man came into the yard just as we were washing at the well.

"Birds!" he shouted.

More men came up behind him. We ran into a barn. There were canoes suspended across the ceiling on hooks, and we climbed up into them, drawing up the ladder behind us. We lay still, scarcely daring to breathe, while the men rushed round the yard like madmen, looking for us and shouting.

Next evening we didn't go near the village, but slept in a hut in the forest. We avoided main roads and people, we were hungry and miserable, and Poland seemed further away than ever. We wondered if we would ever get there. That night Kawka cried softly, just as she had in the camp.

Then at last we reached the River Oder.

An immense, black river, its banks bristling with barbed wire; a large bridge and a narrow foot-bridge. But no one was allowed to go across. We waited there for the whole of one blustery day, cold, exhausted and hungry.

Only when it was quite dark were we allowed across. But why at night? Then we saw what was happening on the other side, and understood instantly . . . bonfires blazing, men chasing women . . . smiling, pretty women, sitting suggestively by the fires, cheeks flaming.

I looked at my group of weary, exhausted girls and saw terror in their eyes. Where were we going to sleep? By this time we were frightened of all men, no matter who they were; soldiers, civilians, Frenchmen, Serbians, Poles or Russians. Not one of those fellows who were looking us over right now, seeing us as just another group of eighteen- to twenty-year-old girls, could have any idea of what we had been through. There was nowhere to go, no barrack huts, nothing but open fields. And those camp-fires, those tents, those eager, groping hands.

I spotted some horses by the water's edge, and we walked towards them. Like a little girl, I spoke to the horse tethered at one end: "Look," I said gently, "take care of us, will you?"

I put Krysia down on a blanket under the horse's belly, and then we all lay down nearby.

The horses stayed quiet and none of them kicked us. But as soon as anyone else came near, they neighed. No one thought of looking for girls underneath the hooves of horses!

Next morning, we continued on our way.

At long last, I don't remember exactly when, we got to Arnswalde, the first railway station in operation since the war. Our feet were torn and bleeding. We sat on the station platform all day waiting for a train. But when one finally steamed in, we were horrified to find it full of men.

Despair. Panic in the girls' eyes. I went to see the station master.

"Sir, we're dying to get home, but we're frightened of those men. We have spent the last four years in a concentration camp longing to be free."

I spoke rapidly, incoherently, not knowing if he understood what I was talking about, or whether he even understood Polish. He looked at me, and when he spoke the relief I felt was immense.

"I have a daughter just like you. Wait here."

He moved off, and walked the whole length of the train before coming back. The carriage to which he escorted us was a goods wagon full of carpets. In it were six soldiers and an officer.

I shall never know what he said to those men, but it was immediately obvious that he had stirred them to pity for us. They were wonderful. They put down carpets for us to sleep on, and even provided us with bedding. They slept in one corner, and we in another. We travelled with them for several days, and for all that time, they treated us with immense tact and sensitivity.

Every time we stopped at a station, 'our boys' – we were soon calling them that – stood blocking the doorway and refusing to let anyone in. During stops, I made soup for us all: the soldiers loved it.

One day well into the journey the officer came and sat next to me. His name was Boris.

"Wanda, what actually happened to you all?" he asked gently.

And I told him the whole sorry story.

Our ways parted at Bydgoszcz, and the boys were sad to see us go.

"Wanda," asked Boris quietly, "would you marry me one day? If we could arrange a meeting in Warsaw, would you accept me?"

I held out my hands towards him. I too spoke quietly:

"Boris, I shall never forget this journey. You have restored my faith in human nature."

Gently he took my hands in his own, and, surprising everyone, including myself, he kissed them. Then he turned on his heel and rapidly walked away.

From Bydgoszcz, we travelled on to Łódź. And then at last we reached Lublin.

Beloved old town! Oh, that marvellous view of the Cathedral from the New Road!

We slowed to a snail's pace. Where were we to go? Where did our families live now? Were they still alive? The suspense was almost unbearable.

An old man was walking along the street, stooping slightly. A familiar figure, but I couldn't quite place him. Running up to him I suddenly remembered. It was our Latin teacher, Jan B. He looked at me with his faded blue eyes, exactly as he had looked in June 1939, when he had danced with me at the school ball.

At sight of me now, he stood still, his face breaking into a huge smile. Holding out his hands, he asked me exactly the same question he had put to me at that dance – in the same tone of voice. It was as though he had seen me only yesterday; as though the intervening years had never been:

"Do you intend to go on and study classics?"

Suddenly I was once again that young girl in school uniform, and I said, smiling just as I had smiled then:

"No, professor, I don't."

He shook his head and spoke the words he had spoken a lifetime ago:

"Pity. It's such an awful waste of talent!"

I kissed his cheek and ran. Yes, ran. All fear had left me. Judging by the expressions on people's faces, I realised I must be doing something extraordinary. And only then did I notice that I was actually using those crippled legs . . . I was actually running!

LUBLIN
28 July 1945

POSTSCRIPT:

RETURN TO RAVENSBRÜCK 1959

On 10 September 1959 a delegation from ZBOWID, the concentration camp survivors' organisation, travelled from Poland to Berlin and from there to Ravensbrück. To be more specific, it was a delegation from the ex-Ravensbrück prisoners' clubs who were to take part in the unveiling of a memorial on the site of the former concentration camp. Even in the train, an unusual nervous tension had been apparent; a jumpiness, an atmosphere in which a single careless word could meet with a violent reaction. The women were palpably on edge, and the nearer the train got to the border and then to Berlin, the more their tension increased.

At East Berlin station, the years fell away in a flash – the uniforms of the German railway officials were exactly the same as they had been in 1945. We got out of the train in an undisciplined scrum, and when a porter pushing a truck-load of suitcases houted "Achtung!" at us, we all jumped. I looked at the woman standing just in front of me: she was actually standing to attention, just as she would have done all those years ago. Stubbornly I made myself look at the heels of her shoes. "Stiletto heels. Stilettos", I kept repeating, trying to reassure myself that those days were indeed over. The moment seemed to last forever.

It was one of our own group who broke the spell by shouting out the once-familiar German words: "Achtung! Bloody women! Idiot people!" Then she burst out laughing. We all followed suit then, but I couldn't help feeling the laughter was a little forced.

Our first night in Berlin.
Four of us are sharing a room. Outside the window

voices can be heard speaking German. None of us sleeps . . .

Ola paces restlessly up and down, smoking cigarette after cigarette, lighting the next one from the previous stub. She continues prowling non-stop, getting on our nerves. "It's just like being in a cell," I thought.

Suddenly she stopped in front of me and shouted:

"Do you know what? I'm frightened! Sheer, bloody frightened! Terrified to death, like an animal, just like it was then! Everything here frightens me . . . Where am I? What am I doing here? What are any of us doing here? What are *you* doing here, and who the hell are you, anyway?" she yelled at me. "For God's sake, don't tell me you're just an ordinary Polish girl."

I didn't answer at first. Then suddenly, still in a state of shock, I spoke woodenly; in words I had said so often before:

"I am prisoner 7709, one of the leg-operation cases!"

Ola burst into loud hysterical laughter and then into tears; then just as suddenly lapsed into silence. In a stifled voice, she asked:

"What the hell did we come here for?"

"We're all getting hysterical," I said, and put out the light. But when morning arrived, none of us had slept, even though we had been silent.

"I just wish we could trust them," said the oldest of the four.

Next day was Saturday. In the morning, coaches festooned with Polish flags took us to Ravensbrück. Along the way small children waved coloured streamers at us; but in the coach there was frozen silence.

And what if it had been my own child standing there waving a flag? I wondered to myself . . .

Someone behind me put the same thought into words:

"Well, anyway, those children are certainly innocent."

And then we all began nodding and waving, stiffly, as though we were mechanical waving machines.

Coaches full of ex-prisoners passed us, waving enthusiastically. Czechs . . . French . . . Norwegians . . . The parade ground was just the same. So was the Bunker. The boundaries that marked off the present from the past began to dissolve, leaving us uncertain of what was real and what was not.

I am outside of time . . . gripped by a mad, irrational fear that at any moment the present will prove to be a dream, and the nightmare past will be the only reality.

I open my eyes wide, close them, open them again, and feel nothing but confusion. I see the woman in front of me pinching her arm hard. I look at the red mark she has made, and think: it's just the same for her . . .

The sight of the gaily-dressed crowd and the colourful flags does nothing to console me; the fear that grips me is more powerful than logic or common sense, and I am drowning in its relentless grasp.

A German voice, seeking to bring order into chaos, shouts:

"Will the Polish delegates stand in rows of five!"

With a single voice we all cry out:

"No! No! Not in rows of five!"

The official looks at us blankly, not understanding. He calls an interpreter who repeats the order:

"The Polish delegates are to stand in rows of five."

And again that single, many-throated cry:

"No! Not in fives!"

They don't understand. In the end I can stand it no longer and shout into the man's ear:

"Man! For five years we stood here in rows of five!"

The penny dropped at last, and he nodded, embarrassed.

We move forward in fours carrying flowers. So very few bunches. We need a whole sea of flowers, there are so many places where we want to strew them.

The monument has been erected beside the lake, and the lake too is just as it was. The edge of the forest looks exactly as it did then . . . We stood in the sweltering heat. I looked round: everyone was lost in thought, their faces suddenly grown hard. Oh God, I thought in sudden terror, they're standing there as if they're at roll-call, waiting to be counted.

The sun was unbelievably hot – as it had so often been all those years ago. Time suddenly fell away.

Then a shot rang out . . . a single, unexpected shot . . . A firing squad! I shivered, as did we all. As we so often had. Only this time there was no need. They were just shooting flares into the sky, many-hued streamers that mingled their brilliant colours with the sun.

Wiesia mounted the platform. She was fourteen and had been born in Ravensbrück. She was supposed to make a little speech, but when she opened her mouth, she burst into tears.

A woman standing just behind me broke into loud, racking, hysterical sobs. That struck me as being so alien and melodramatic that I shuddered with distaste. Who was it? I wondered. Surely it couldn't have been one of our group! I looked round. It was our interpreter, the one who, when we had asked her the previous day if she was a native of Berlin, had replied: "Once, until 1945 in fact, I too was Polish . . ."

Someone seized me by the hand:

"Come on, the press want to talk to you."

We pushed our way through the brightly-coloured, polyglot crowd, looking for 'the press'. A young blonde girl hailed me and laboriously wrote down the letters of my name before putting her first question:

"You were operated on? What did they do to you? To all of you, but specifically to you?"

I was silent, remembering a voice from the past that had asked those same questions: What did they do to you? What are they going to do to us all? What will become of us? – I heard again the strangled, terrified voice of Marysia Gnaś: "What do you think will become of us?"

On a blazing hot day just like this one, in this very place, on this self-same square, we had stood in row. They had taken us first to HQ and then to the rewir, and Marysia, that big, strapping country lass, had gone on asking over and over again: "What will they do to us? What will they do?"

And I heard my own voice answering with a word which had rarely till then figured in my vocabulary: "Exterminate us."

I remembered how that word shook me even then, how I noticed that Marysia's flushed and rosy face had gone grey, her eyes turning black as the pupils had dilated. She hadn't said another word after that, but I could hear her teeth chattering. Really chattering, knocking against each other noisily.

"Why aren't I afraid like her?" I had wondered in surprise. "Why aren't I weeping for my 'lost youth'? Why aren't I examining my conscience or singing the Marseillaise or something?" I was so unnaturally calm that I began to wonder if I was quite normal. How could I go to meet death with such indifference? It wasn't right.

But when I thought about it, I realised that the answer was quite simple: I just couldn't convince myself that I was going to die, and that was why I wasn't afraid. I smiled then, and my smile seemed to reassure Marysia because she stopped trembling.

Sister Frieda had come out of the rewir and ordered us to clean up in the bathroom. I had felt angry at what I thought was a new piece of play-acting. Before this, they used always to give a piece of bread to condemned prisoners, making believe they were going on a journey. The bread had always come back with their bloodstained dresses. But *we* were being given a bath instead of bread. The stupid idiots!

All the same, I had enjoyed that bath. "Look how clean you're going to be when you die," I had said jokingly to Marysia. And again I had been startled by her reaction. She went green and vomited over the side of the bath.

When I had asked the orderly what was going on, she bent over and whispered: "They're going to operate on you."

Stupid woman, what was she talking about, I remember thinking. We were young and healthy. "The silly cow's afraid to tell us the truth," I thought – as it happened, aloud!

Then they had taken us to that little end room with its clean white beds. And that in itself had been extraordinary, since it was a long time since we had seen any sheets.

I had come straight from the night-shift, and announced with the sublime unconcern of youth that it was almost worth dying if you could sleep in a clean bed before you went.

But Marysia had not let me sleep. She had perched on the end of the bed, asking that endless circular question: "What are they going to do to us? Please, Wanda, please, tell me what they're going to do."

Zielonkowa, the oldest, had prayed the Rosary aloud. Rózia, the youngest, sixteen years old, had cried quietly to herself.

Sister Frieda had returned to give us all an injection. I did not offer any resistance. "At least they're doing it in style," I had thought. "Putting us down humanely; with dignity. No blood, no salvo of guns." And even then I felt no fear.

But the injection had not killed us, it had simply left us in the grip of a paralysing inertia. '

"Jesus, what are they doing to us?" poor Marysia still asked. "What does it all mean?'

Sister Frieda had returned with a razor. Marysia had shrieked and pulled the bedspread up over her head. Wanda, sitting nearest the door, had gone as white as the wall when the nurse approached with the razor. I had stared, transfixed, as the nurse shaved Wanda's legs.

Zielonkowa had interrupted her 'Hail Marys' to say in a voice quite unlike her normal one: "Dear God, just let them kill us, just kill us." (They *did* kill her, but that was later.)

Marysia had emerged from the bedspread and was silently opening and shutting her mouth like a stranded fish.

Suddenly I thought of the electrified wire outside. The

window was open, the wire was just outside, the high-tension wire that could release me.

I had tensed myself quietly, getting ready to spring out of the window. But when Frieda had turned her back and I had tried to jump, I had fallen back limply on to the bed. My legs had turned to cotton-wool. They were quite useless.

And what was it that we had cried on the operating table, our last defiant cry? "We are not guinea-pigs to be experimented on." Not guinea-pigs!

And now the German girl was asking that very thing: in the same place some fifteen years later.

I pulled myself together . . . She repeated the question, this time more impatiently:

"And what did they do to you personally?"

I looked more closely at her then asked, perhaps a shade too emphatically:

"Are you telling me you really don't know about the Ravensbrück experiments?"

She was clearly embarrassed and spoke quickly:

"Well, naturally I've read and heard something about them."

"Well, they did the same to me as they did to all the others. Do you know what that was?"

She hesitated a moment before asking:

"Why did you all come back?"

I stared at her. Why indeed? How could I explain about all those who had lived out their last lonely moments in this place? Nothing could take away the fact of that last terrible loneliness. None of us would ever know what their feelings had been then, those who had remained here for ever. And yet I could have told you so much else about each one of them: that Pola was slim and Grażyna had blonde curls, that Halina had amber-coloured eyes, that Niusia was always discontented, while Romka always smiled. Most of all I could have told you about little Mila, the last one to arrive in our prison cell in Lublin. Tiny, with huge eyes and a little bird-like nose, she had sat on the edge of her wooden bed, coughing her heart out. It was very crowded and Krysia and I were sleeping on a narrow table, tied on with a belt so that we wouldn't fall off. I got up and gave her some cough medicine from Niusia's supplies, saying: "Come on, little pigeon, have some of this." And after that I would always call her 'pigeon' or 'little one', although actually she was older than me. I remember how she sat in a corner and told us she'd been arrested "because they couldn't find Janek". She kept showing us her palm and saying: "Look what a short life-line I've got. I shall die soon. But I shan't be afraid if I can be with you or Pola." Then came news that Janek had been arrested and I woke in the night to find Mila wide awake, sitting up and weeping softly. I sat by her and called her 'little pigeon', just as I'd done on the night of her arrival.

When she went to her death, it was with Pola, but not with me . . . on just such a hot day as this. Before going, she came to me with the final request: "Give my love to the meadows at home, and tell my mother that I wasn't afraid." She had always told me that those meadows in bloom were the most beautiful place on earth . . .

She had gone, and when she was already some distance away had turned and waved us a last goodbye. Here, on this square, on a day so very long ago.

What had Mila felt in those last lonely moments?

I *did* go to those meadows of hers, the first Sunday of my return. They were in bloom and were just as beautiful as she had described. I saw the path leading to the mill and walked slowly down it. "An old woman will come out of the mill," I thought. "She will be tiny like Mila, and with Mila's eyes. She will ask me where her daughter is. And how can I tell her that I came back but her daughter did not?"

And now, back in the present, how could I tell this blonde German woman that I'd run back across the meadow with Mila's last request unfulfilled: that that was why I had come back to Ravensbrück. To apologise to Mila for funking what she had asked me to do?

I tore myself away from those flower-strewn meadows

and forced myself to concentrate. The woman was still standing there, but I didn't say a word.

She shrank back. Indeed, literally so: her head seeming to retract into her shoulders.

"Will you excuse me, please."

With that she turned and went quickly away, too quickly for comfort. Just like me when I had fled from Mila's parents, I thought.

I too turned and walked away. Under my feet the same black coal dust, nothing had changed at all. One day, just before the end, Krysia and I had walked along there, carrying a cauldron of soup. Goldstücks had rushed at us and snatched the cauldron from our grasp, spilling the soup on to this black coal dust. And then they had fallen to the ground and licked up soup and dust together. An overseer had come up, lashing out, striking indiscriminately at arms, heads, backs with her whip. But the Goldstücks had gone on licking, until all that had remained was a damp patch in the dust.

We had watched helplessly. The overseer pointed to the cauldron and shouted to us to take it away, at the double. We picked it up, but had had to stop before long because it was too heavy. "But it's empty," I thought, "so how can it be so heavy?" Krysia read my thoughts: "Do you remember, when we first went to block 15 we used to carry a full cauldron all the way from the kitchen to the block without stopping once? And now we have to stop every couple of steps with an empty one!"

Krysia was right. I looked at her. She was pale and painfully thin. The striped uniform hung off her as if from a clothes peg. In sudden fury I bent down to pick up the cauldron – and banged my leg on it. The pain nearly took my breath away. Someone grabbed my arm, and I thought for a moment that it was the overseer. But it was the friendly, cheerful Hanka B. "What's the matter?" she asked. "Is your leg hurting again?"

And suddenly I realised where I was. For Hanka was wearing a pretty white blouse, and there was not a cauldron in sight. But she was right, my leg *was* hurting.

186

"I think I must have been standing too long," I said.

1960. A year has gone by, and once again I am in Berlin. Once again the sun shines down fiercely and I am gripped by the old familiar terror.

The third Sunday of September is dedicated to the victims of fascism. Hundreds of wreaths, great mounds of flowers, row after row of young people and adults placing those tributes on the graves of their dead and on the earth once occupied by the concentration camps.

Once again there is a Polish delegation, not many of us this time, just a few. Five proud possessors of the 'Enemy of Fascism' medal.

I decide that the time has come to get rid of this instinctive fear of Germans; and I resolve to put aside my memories of Ravensbrück.

We walk round museums . . . visit art galleries . . . see everything there is to see . . . visit hospitals and look at people.

I peer into prams: exactly the same round baby faces . . . the women just as careworn. Slowly, I relax and manage to smile at these people . . . And they smile back.

At last I seemed to be making progress. One day in the street, I found myself talking quite naturally to a mother standing with a push-chair: "Oh dear – the little fellow's got whooping cough!" The child, aged about two, had a hacking cough, and I really did feel sorry for his mother too . . .

That same day, I had lunch with someone who asked if I was enjoying Berlin. "D'you know," I said slowly, carefully, "I think I'm at last beginning to believe that the Poles and the Germans can be friends."

Leon looked plainly delighted: "Well," he said. "The trip will have been worthwhile if only for that, if even *one* person has been converted."

We drove on to Sachsenhausen – again it was a lovely sunny day. We saw the museum which was still being built and wandered around the site of the former camp. On what had once been Death Row, a red rose bush was in bloom. It bore a small card announcing that someone's daughter had planted the roses in memory of her mother.

I dreamed of the rose bush that night. It was just as I had seen it earlier in the day, and the weather was just the same – baking hot sunshine. Five of us were standing in line by that bush – and suddenly I went cold all over. I shivered . . . turned round . . . and froze to the spot. There on Death Row stood five SS men, their rifles pointing directly at us. And then it came to me: so that was why we had each received a personal invitation to visit Sachsenhausen.

I must have cried out in my sleep, for Senka shook me gently awake. Stroking my hand, she asked what the matter was.

I snapped straight out of the nightmare.

"It's nothing. Just another dream that they were going to shoot us."

Senka covered me carefully with the quilt.

"Your breath was coming so quickly that I knew I'd better wake you," she said. "My husband often cried out in his sleep, just like that . . ."

AUTHOR'S POSTSCRIPT 1986

1 March 1986, Hotel Michelangelo, Rome. International Right To Life Congress.

"Whatever's the matter? What's happened?" asked my friend sharply.

"Don't worry, it's nothing." (Well, nothing to speak of . . . and anyway, how could I explain?) "I won't even try to explain. Nobody would understand."

It was the last day of the congress; I had given my report, and now, in a luxury hotel with soft, comfortable armchairs, I could discuss the proceedings with a host of new acquaintances. Interesting people, with interesting things to talk about . . .

Over in a corner by a wall were some long rectangular tables laden with a great variety of books. Groups from many different countries had brought their own literature to put on display. I wandered over, glanced at the books and prospectuses, bought one or two. Suddenly my attention was caught by a small booklet with a turbaned genie on the cover. Its title, *Release*, gave me no clue as to its contents, and the smaller print that followed was puzzling: 'of the destruction of life devoid of value'. Whatever could it mean?

I began leafing through it – and suddenly, on page 85, I saw a photograph which I recognised: a leg, Jadzia Dzido's leg, to be precise. Jadzia Dzido, who had in fact died a month earlier, had been a fellow-prisoner in Ravensbrück, and, like me, had been experimented on. There was no face, but I knew that the leg was hers. The other leg in the picture was Czesia Kostecka's.

On the last page of all, page 111, I saw a full-length picture of Marysia Kusmierczuk which showed her mutilated and deformed legs. The photograph, which did not identify Marysia by name, had been taken during the War Crimes Trials at Nuremberg.

Then, on page 88, a face which hundreds of times in the last forty-five years had haunted my sleep. 'Dr Karl Gebhardt of Hohenlychen Hospital, Berlin', the picture informed me – and suddenly I could once again see that man leaning over me, saying, "Now, here's a fine young girl" – while someone behind him whispered, "Psst, that one understands German." Once again, I could feel Dr Gebhardt – in that place they had called him Professor – examining my mangled leg.

I closed the book, then opened it again. All of a sudden the brightly lit room went dark, and I made a hasty, unseeing exit.

How could I have explained to my conference colleagues – that certain memories will for ever retain their original vivid intensity! I recognised the symptoms; I had even written a paper about this type of 'aggressive hypermnesia', in which some outside trigger sets in motion a sequence of images that are fixed in the memory for all time, like a film waiting to be shown.

No, nothing had actually happened. But I didn't sleep that night. Was it that I *couldn't*, or was I terrified of the dreams that might come? And, difficult though it may be to believe, I was plagued all night long by pain in my leg. Just as in the old days.

Perhaps that was why, immediately after the congress, I accepted an invitation to another congress, to be held in May 1986 at Hadamar in the Federal German Republic; I forced myself to go back there again. This congress, held in protest against the murder of stateless babies, innocent, defenceless babies, had chosen Hadamar as its symbolic venue. For it was in the psychiatric hospital at Hadamar that the Nazis had once murdered ten thousand mentally-ill patients. And now once again the arguments for euthanasia were making themselves heard.

Beneath the photograph of Dr Gebhardt in the booklet

were the words: 'He was hanged.' He was hanged precisely because of the things I have written about – my own mutilated leg and those of Jadzia Dzido and all the other 'guinea-pigs' of Ravensbrück. Today once again there are doctors who have been given life-or-death powers over the human embryo, who even perform experiments on living embryos. Yet no one stands in judgment on *them*.

I was at that congress in Germany as the representative of the Pope's Commission For The Family, together with Bishop Tschidimbo. But on that occasion I was also representing myself. When my turn came to report, I said: "I want to tell you exactly why I have come to this place, exactly why these issues concern me so greatly." Then, for the first time in forty-five years, the very first time, of my own free will I told that gathering of people just why it had taken me so long to return to West Germany. Speaking in German, I said, just as I had said during roll-call in the camp:

"I am prisoner number 7709."

And now the letters are beginning to come in. One person has written to ask for forgiveness in the name of the German nation, and swears that, though she used to live near that very hospital in Hadamar, she had not known what had happened there. But *I* knew and know only too well. And if once again I have sleepless nights, perhaps some of you may understand why.

ABOUT THE AUTHOR

Wanda Półtawska became a doctor after World War II and went on to study psychiatry and specialize in the treatment of juvenile patients, including the deeply-traumatized "Auschwitz children." She worked in the psychiatric clinic of Krakow's Medical Academy and at Jagiellonian University in Poland. She was also a close friend and advisor to Pope John Paul II, serving on the Papal Commission on Family Matters. Married with four daughters, Półtawska resides in her native Poland.

ABOUT THE TRANSLATOR

Mary Craig is an experienced journalist, broadcaster and highly-acclaimed author. Her bestelling autobiography *Blessings* is an inspirational account of raising two handicapped children. She has also authored biographies of Pope John Paul II and Lech Wałesa.

Also available from Hippocrene Books

POLAND: A HISTORY
Adam Zamoyski

"Excellent and authoritative...Such an extraordinary national trajectory demands an accessible and scholarly accounting. Zamoyski succeeds admirably in providing both."
—The Daily Telegraph

Adam Zamoyski's bestselling first history of Poland, *The Polish Way*, was released in 1987 when the country was in a state of subjugation, with most of its living culture surviving underground or in exile. As he set out to update his original work, he realized the task required not so much re-writing as re-thinking the known facts as well as the assumptions of the past. The events of the last twenty years and the growth of the independent Polish state allowed him to look at Poland's past with a fresh eye.

Poland: A History traces Poland's complex development from the Middle Ages to present day, examining the country's political, economic, and military struggles, as well as its culture, art, and richly varied society through the ages. Zamoyski brings the major events and characters in Poland's history to life.

Adam Zamoyski was born in New York and has spent much of his life in England, where he was educated at Oxford. His family originates from Poland, which his parents fled when it was invaded by Germany and Russia in 1939. A historian with a singular command of languages, he has authored over a dozen books. He is married to the painter Emma Sargeant and resides in England.

ISBN 978-0-7818-1301-3 · $19.95pb

FORGOTTEN HOLOCAUST: THE POLES UNDER GERMAN OCCUPATION, 1939-1944
Third Edition
Richard Lukas

- A classic of World War II literature, *Forgotten Holocaust*, has been revised and updated. The third edition includes:
- A new preface by the author
- A new foreword by Norman Davies
- A short history of *ZEGOTA*, the underground government organization working to save the Jews
- An annotated listing of many Poles executed by the Germans for trying to shelter and save Jews

Richard C. Lukas has authored and co-authored nine books including *Did the Children Cry?* with Hippocrene Books (1994 and 2001). He earned his Ph.D. in history from Florida State University, and in recognition of his scholarship, Alliance College granted him the honorary degree of Doctor of Humane Letters in 1987. He currently resides in Florida.

ISBN 978-0-7818-1302-0 · $19.95pb

Prices subject to change without prior notice. **To purchase Hippocrene Books** contact your local bookstore, visit www.hippocrenebooks.com, call (212) 685-4373, or write to: HIPPOCRENE BOOKS, 171 Madison Avenue, New York, NY 10016.